Identity, Education and Belonging

MUP ISLAMIC STUDIES SERIES

The Islamic Studies Series (ISS) is aimed at producing internationally competitive research manuscripts. This series will showcase the breadth of scholarship on Islam and Muslim affairs, making it available to a wide readership. Books in the ISS are based on original research and represent a number of disciplines including anthropology, cultural studies, sociology and political science. Books in the ISS are refereed publications that are committed to research excellence. Submissions on contemporary issues are strongly encouraged. Proposals should be sent to the ISS Editor.

Associate Professor Shahram Akbarzadeh
ISS Editor (shahrama@unimelb.edu.au)

Board of Advisors

Associate Professor Syed Farid Alatas
Department of Sociology, National University of Singapore

Professor Howard V. Brasted
School of Humanities, University of New England

Professor Robert E. Elson
School of History, Philosophy, Religion and Classics, University of Queensland

Professor John Esposito
Director, Prince Alwaleed bin Talal Center for Muslim-Christian Understanding, University Professor of Religion and International Affairs, Georgetown University

Emeritus Professor Riaz Hassan AM, FASSA
ARC Australian Professorial Fellow, Department of Sociology, Flinders University

Professor Robert Hefner
Institute on Culture, Religion and World Affairs, Boston University

Professor Michael Humphrey
Chair, Department of Sociology and Social Policy, School of Philosophical and Historical Inquiry, University of Sydney

Professor William Maley AM
Director, Asia-Pacific College of Diplomacy, Australian National University

Professor James Piscatori
Centre for Arab and Islamic Studies (The Middle East and Central Asia), Australian National University

Professor Abdullah Saeed
Sultan of Oman Professor of Arab and Islamic Studies, Director, National Centre of Excellence for Islamic Studies, University of Melbourne

Professor Amin Saikal AM
Director, Centre for Arab and Islamic Studies (The Middle East and Central Asia), Australian National University

Associate Professor Samina Yasmeen
Director, Centre for Muslim States and Societies, School of Social and Cultural Studies, University of Western Australia

Identity, Education and Belonging

Arab and Muslim youth in contemporary Australia

Fethi Mansouri

&

Sally Percival Wood

MELBOURNE UNIVERSITY PRESS
An imprint of Melbourne University Publishing Limited
187 Grattan Street, Carlton, Victoria 3053, Australia
mup-info@unimelb.edu.au
www.mup.com.au

First published 2008
Text © Fethi Mansouri and Sally Percival Wood, 2008
Design and typography © Melbourne University Publishing Limited, 2008

Designed by Phil Campbell
Typeset by J & M Typesetting
Printed and bound by CPI Group (UK) Ltd, Croydon, CR0 4YY

National Library of Australia Cataloguing-in-Publication entry:

Mansouri, Fethi, 1967–

Identity, education and belonging: Arab and Muslim youth in contemporary Australia / Fethi Mansouri and Sally Wood.

9780522856767 (pdf.)
9780522856774 (pbk.)

Includes index.
Bibliography.

Identity (Psychology) in youth — Australia.
Muslim youth — Australia — Attitudes.
Arabs — Australia — Attitudes.
Culture conflict — Australia — History — 21st century.

Wood, Sally (Sally Percival)

305.2350994

Contents

List of Figures

Acknowledgments

This book is the result of a number of projects that dealt with Arab and Muslim youth in Australian schools, Muslim asylum seekers in contemporary Australia, multicultural education, the settlement patterns of Arab Australian communities and intercultural adaptation among migrant youth. These projects were supported by a number of grants from Deakin University, the Telstra Foundation, the Scanlon Foundation (formerly the Brencorp Foundation), the William Buckland Foundation and a major grant from the Australian Research Council. We are grateful to this ongoing support that enabled these projects to be conducted and provide the basis for the various parts of this book. A number of external partnerships have also facilitated the completion of this research most notably that with the Victorian Arabic Social Services to whom we are grateful for building strong partnerships with a number of schools in the northern and western regions of Melbourne. We would also like to acknowledge the input and support of other colleagues who contributed to this wide ranging research agenda in particular Michael Leach, Louise Jenkins, Lucas Walsh, Annelies Kamp, Loretta Duffy, Anna Trembath and Michelle Miller. We are also grateful to the professional support provided by MUP and in particular the series commissioning editor A/Professor Shahram Akbarzadeh. Finally, we would like to express our deepest gratitude to the hundreds of students, parents, teachers and other school leaders who played an essential part in the successful completion of these projects. We hope this book will assist modestly in providing a better understanding of their educational and social experiences.

Fethi Mansouri and Sally Percival Wood
Melbourne, October 2008

Introduction

Arab and Muslim Australians in the
Current Socio-political Context

In the aftermath of the September 11 attacks and the subsequent 'war on terror', a heated debate resurfaced on the place of Arab and Muslim migrants in Australian society. The debate reflects contemporary concerns about security issues and migration policies, concerns shared by other Western societies, but also indicates a longstanding uneasiness and ambivalence towards Muslim and Arab presence in Australia.

The fact that the perpetrators of the terrorist attacks in New York and Washington were Muslims, that asylum seekers across the last decade have been predominantly Muslim, and that more recent Australian military engagement has been primarily in Muslim countries, has meant that in the public mind 'Muslims' are at least synonymous with immediate threats if not considered outright enemies. That information on these complex issues is mostly filtered through the media has not helped Australians either in their understanding of Islam or of the Muslim experience. One of the clear problems emanating from the media and public discourses that have been generated since September 11 is the simplistic overgeneralisation of Muslims and Arabs who come from diverse linguistic and cultural backgrounds and often hold varying interpretations of

Islamic beliefs that go beyond the well publicised Sunni–Shia schism. Such generalisations can be difficult to overcome, as they involve a complex coalescence of national, ethnic, cultural and linguistic factors. While this book acknowledges this as implicit, for the sake of linguistic and stylistic simplicity the term 'Arab and Muslim Australians' will be used throughout to refer to all participants in the research that it reports. However, in some cases there will be distinct references and comments that relate specifically to Muslims and Islam in the context of wider societal and political discussions.

Historically Muslim Australians have faced considerable cultural and political obstacles in their attempts to fully integrate into Australian society. These obstacles have been made all the more challenging in a political climate dominated by security and terrorism concerns. Recent international events, such as the war between Israel and Lebanon, the ongoing conflict in Iraq, Australia's increased military presence in Afghanistan, and the nuclear 'threat' of Iran, maintain a steady focus on the instability and unpredictability of the Muslim world. Together with domestic events, such as the arrival of (largely Muslim) onshore asylum seekers and the Cronulla riots, race-driven politics linking Arab and Muslim Australians negatively to global politics and 'national security' concerns are reinforced. In this context, national security has become a concept that generates anxiety and fear that the 'other', predominantly from the Middle East—mainly Muslim migrants and refugees—might act in a hostile way. As governments all over the world argue, 'Because such anxieties are easily aroused and because they can easily be directed against any domestic or foreign group that is labelled a threat, worry about national security is constantly evoked.'[1] National security can, therefore, be used to articulate and legitimate racial and religious misrepresentations against minority groups with impunity. The national paranoia that followed 'national security' issues, such as the 'war on terror' and 'border protection', resulted in a racialised, exclusionary discourse of demonisation, misrepresentation and mistrust aimed at Australians of Muslim and Arabic backgrounds.

In July 2007, the front page of *The Australian* newspaper warned against the 'home-grown jihad threat' in Australia's largest city, Sydney.[2] The report, based on government-funded investigations undertaken by hand-picked Muslim 'community leaders', claimed that up to 3000 young Muslim Australians in Sydney alone 'are at risk of being radicalised by fundamentalist Islam'.[3] This revelation coincided with the arrest in Lebanon of five Australian-Lebanese men over alleged links to Fatah-Al-Islam, a group that has been locked in armed confrontation with the Lebanese Army. Also in July 2007, Australia tested its 'terrorist legislation' for the first time when an Indian-born Muslim, Dr Mohamed Haneef, was apprehended at Brisbane Airport and subsequently held for eleven days without charge. Dr Haneef was questioned over the failed bomb plots in Glasgow and London and finally arrested on charges of recklessly giving a mobile phone SIM card to a relative in the UK who was later suspected of involvement in the failed bomb attacks. The ongoing trial of 'Jihad' Jack Thomas for alleged links with Al-Qaeda has also served to demonise Islam as a religion, or way of life, incompatible with 'Australianness'. In each instance, these revelations affirm anxieties that the threat of radical Islam has permeated Australian society, but equally they expose the potential of the 'war on terror' to undermine the viability of Australia as a multicultural society. The case against Dr Haneef was later dropped as the prosecution could not pursue the charges against him and the charges against Jack Thomas were quashed.

Amid claims of hardline Muslim clerics exploiting community divisions, and assertions that Australia's relatively new encounter with Islam made it vulnerable to radicalisation, media coverage of these events seemed to cement Australia's links with global terrorist networks, intensifying its domestic vulnerability. The common thread binding these various security incidents is that the protagonists are all young Muslim men either residing or born in the West. This raises the now familiar question of the extent to which Muslim migrants are able to integrate into Western secular societies, such as Australia. But media reporting of social and political events is not confined to Muslim professionals linked to or engaged in political and ideological confrontations. In fact, Arab and Muslim Australian youth studying in state schools are occasionally referred to in similar terms.

Three years ago in Melbourne, Australia's second-largest city, the media alerted the public to what it called Lebanese 'thugs' and 'ethnic gangs' that were infiltrating and corrupting schools in the city's north-western suburbs. Indeed, in July 2004, a public secondary

school in the northern suburbs of Melbourne announced its immi-
nent closure.[4] Moreland City College (MCC), located in the heart of
one of Melbourne's most socio-economically disadvantaged communities, had served a culturally and linguistically diverse student
population, only 20 per cent of whom were from English-speaking
backgrounds and more than 50 per cent from Arabic-speaking backgrounds.[5] MCC enrolments had been dropping steadily for a number
of years, and its students' average educational attainments fell significantly below Victorian state averages. At the time the closure was
announced, it was common knowledge that a variety of complex and
interlinked factors contributed to the school's demise. A legacy of
school 'economic rationalisation' in Victoria in the 1990s, MCC was
created through the amalgamation of a number of schools in the
area. By 2004 however, it was publicly argued that MCC lacked the
requisite government support and funding resources to ensure the
effective integration of students originating from different educational institutions. This lack of adequate resources meant that the
school was unable to provide its diverse student cohorts with curriculum choices to meet their varied educational needs and interests.[6]

In addition to this insufficiently resourced structural change,
MCC became publicly embroiled in the complex politics of Australian
multiculturalism in the post–September 11 environment. Drawn into
this highly security-conscious context, the issue was further exacerbated when a prominent tabloid journalist[7] argued that the school
had become a 'sour ethnic ghetto' dominated by Arab and Muslim
Australian students and their families, and was home to violent
Lebanese 'ethnic gangs'.[8] After the announcement of the school's
closure, the same journalist wrote that Moreland City College had
been 'killed by ethnic division', contending that multicultural educational policies had resulted in a 'too-heavy concentration of Muslim
students, particularly Lebanese[9]', 'trapping immigrant students in
their own closed culture' and leading to a rejection of Australia and
its core values.[10] As a consequence of this negative media depiction,
the school acquired a reputation for being educationally ineffective,
isolated from mainstream Australian society, and serving only one
ethnic group constructed in populist media discourse as criminal,
deviant and threatening. At the time of the announcement that the
school would be closed, even the Victorian Opposition spokesman

for education echoed the media's negative representations, arguing that the Government had failed to intervene in a school that was a 'hot-bed of violence and thuggery'.[11] The closure of the Moreland City College is a reminder that sustainable educational success cannot be taken for granted. It also highlights the ongoing need for innovative approaches to teaching in culturally diverse schools, wherein quality education—with systematic multicultural perspectives—would be viewed as a basic right, and an essential means, to social cohesion and economic development.

Against this tense socio-political climate, this book locates the social and educational experiences of Arab and Muslim Australian youth within wider national and global events. It seeks to explore the cultural attitudes, social insecurities and educational experiences of Arab and Muslim Australian students at two secondary schools in Melbourne's north-western region. It does so by exploring how Arab and Muslim Australian students at state schools understand and construct their own social and educational experiences. The study also considers parents' and teachers' perspectives on the politics of educational achievements in an attempt to paint as holistic a picture as possible of the perceived challenges posed by multiculturalism. Though the sampling is small, the purpose here is to shed light on the lived experience of young Arab and Muslim Australians in a typical community and educational setting, a perspective that is often obfuscated by fears of the grander narrative of global terrorism. The study argues that at a time when Arab and Muslim communities in Australia are sometimes represented as the 'pre-eminent folk devil[12]', critical links may exist between their perceptions of belonging, identity and citizenship on the one hand, and their attitudes to schooling and educational experiences on the other. The findings of the study sit within an historical trajectory that begins with the history of Australian attitudes towards Muslim migrants, to the contemporary effects of socio-political trends of marginalisation and negative stereotyping upon the educational experiences of Arab and Muslim youth in Australia.

To explore this rather vast theme, Chapter 1 begins with an historical analysis of the settlement of Muslim migrants from the pre-Federation era and their early encounter with social prejudice and cultural denigration. It then traces the changing fortunes of

Muslim migrants in Australia as global events, most notably World Wars I and II, increased perceptions of their unsuitability for successful integration into an otherwise 'white' Australia. This chapter moves on to the discussion of multiculturalism as a state-sanctioned social policy in the 1970s and discusses its mixed record of successfully facilitating the settlement of migrants from non-English-speaking background, but also highlights its shortcomings and its current ambiguous status. Chapter 2 focuses on the educational experiences of Arab and Muslim Australian youth as reported in a growing body of academic research. The initial argument developed in this chapter is that schooling experience plays a crucial role not only in shaping students' economic prospects but also in their identity formation. Hence, there is a need to ensure that teaching approaches and curriculum resources are inclusive of diverse student cultures. The chapter reports on and discusses a number of studies carried out that looked into the educational attainments of students from Arab and Muslim backgrounds, highlighting the need to steer away from assumptions of a possible correlation between ethnicity and educational performance. Chapters 1 and 2 thus provide a socio-historical background to the experiences of Arabs and Muslims in Australia, moving towards a more particular understanding of youth that is identified in the research discussed in Chapters 3 and 4.

Chapter 3 reports on a longitudinal study that investigated the management of cultural diversity in secondary schools. The study was motivated by gaps in existing pedagogical approaches and curricular responses to multicultural education. It argues that in order to improve the educational achievements of migrant youth, in particular those of Arab and Muslim backgrounds, a multidimensional partnership model needs to be adopted by schools, with community organisations and parents also engaging in meaningful and effective collaboration. This reflects the study's theoretical approach that is underpinned by critical educational theories and critical race theory. This perspective posits that school ideologies and deep 'hidden' structures can be challenged and, where necessary, reformed through holistic partnerships and collaborations. Chapter 4 is also based on the empirical study reported in this book but focuses specifically on the lived experiences of Arab and Muslim Australian students in the wider mainstream society. The attitudes of students, parents and teachers reported in this section confirm the fluid and challenging nature of multicultural schools. Of particular concern here is the level of awareness among students of the pervasive political debates about terrorism, border control and identity politics. This indeed builds a more compelling case for ongoing and proactive monitoring of school structures to ensure equity and transparency within inclusive cosmopolitan curricula.

Chapter 5 locates these findings within their wider social contexts and discusses their implications for policy and practice. One of the more worrying aspects of this study's findings relates to the fact that Arab and Muslim Australian students are more likely to express distrust towards teachers than other students because of a perceived lack of cultural understanding. It is this intercultural tension, both within schools and beyond their confines, that risks damage to social cohesion in contemporary Australian society. This empirical study, with its emphasis on partnership and holistic intervention strategies, provides an example of how to build stronger school communities in a sustainable manner.

Woven into the broader perspective of the experience of Arab and Muslim Australian youth are the findings of the project undertaken in the northern metropolitan region of Melbourne. The *Diversity Project* investigated the challenges posed by cultural diversity in multicultural schools. It focused specifically on Year 9 and 10 students and their families attending secondary schools in order to gauge whether individual students' motivations, parents' attitudes, schools' structures and teachers' pedagogical approaches, as well as curricular composition, impact upon Arab and Muslim Australian students' educational achievements and sense of social belonging.

The study provides fresh empirical data on the inter-related questions of race relations, racialised representation of minority groups, and the possible impact of such phenomena on students' overall attitudes towards schooling and social integration. To better situate these debates in the wider literature, Chapter 6 reflects on recent debates in Australia about multiculturalism as a social project and as a theoretical construct, and discusses the role of the media in shaping public perceptions of Arab and Muslim Australians.

Notes

1   M Edelman, 2001, *The Politics of Disinformation*, Cambridge University Press, Cambridge, p. 7.
2   R Kerbaj and M Chulov, 2007, 'Australia's Home-Grown Jihad Threat', *The Australian*, p. 1, 2 July.
3   ibid.
4   For details on this incident please refer to Fethi Mansouri and Anna Trembath, 2005, 'Multicultural Education and Racism: The Case of Arab-Australian Students in Contemporary Australia', *International Education Journal*, vol. 6, no. 4, pp. 516–29.
5   Student Outcomes Division, Department of Education & Training, 2003, *Annual Report 2002*, State of Victoria, Melbourne; see also Student Outcomes Division, Department of Education & Training 2004, *2004 School Census: Language Background Other Than English Student*, State of Victoria, Melbourne.
6   K Echberg, 2004, 'Sad End to a School with a Proud and Vibrant Past', *The Age*, 4 August; see also S Green, 2004, 'Troubled School Shuts Door', *The Age*, 31 July; and Editorial, 2004, 'Sacrificing Schools to the Numbers Game', *The Age*, 4 August.
7   A Bolt, 2002, 'Schooled to Fail', *Herald Sun*, 16 December.
8   A Bolt, 2004, 'A Culture in Crisis, *Herald Sun*, 15 September; see also A Bolt 2004, 'Moaners Strangle a School', *Herald Sun*, 1 August.
9   ibid.
10 ibid.
11 *Herald Sun*, 2004, 'School Closure "Right Thing to Do"', 31 July.
12 S Poynting, G Noble, P Tabar and J Collins, 2004, '*Bin Laden in the Suburbs: Criminalising the Arab Other*', Sydney Institute of Criminology Series, Sydney.

Chapter 1

Multiculturalism, the Media and Muslims in Australia

The presence of Muslims in Australia, and the West in general, and debates about their readiness to integrate into Western societies is presupposed on an assumption that the Islamic encounter with the West is a postcolonial phenomenon. Closer scrutiny of Islam's expansion beyond the modern contours of the Middle East and North Africa reveals that the Muslim faith and its adherents not only spread into Central and Southeast Asia, but also into southern Europe and northward into the Balkans. Indeed, Islam has interacted with the West for as many centuries as Christianity has with the East. Similarly, Australia, albeit with only two centuries of Anglo-European settlement, has been influenced by Muslim migration from its formative days.[1] In fact, Australia has a long history of Muslim settlement, beginning with the arrival of thousands of Afghan cameleers who came to help European pioneers open up the 'Red Centre' in the mid-nineteenth century. These Afghan Muslims were Australia's first victims of what is now called 'Islamophobia'.[2] As early as the latter parts of the nineteenth century, Afghans were the subject of a major racist campaign stemming from tensions with Anglo-Australian bullock drivers. Lebanese immigration to Australia also began quite early, in the 1870s and 1880s, though these early Lebanese immigrants identified themselves as Syrians.[3] They were similarly vilified, and in 1898, through a public campaign supported by the Melbourne *Leader* newspaper, Syrian and Indian hawkers in capital cities were subjected to accusations of criminality, disease, and of bullying housewives.

After Federation in 1901, Australia's first legislative move was the *Immigration Restriction Act* (or 'White Australia Policy', as it was famously known), which formalised the exclusion of non-European— and non-Christian—migrants. Immigration and citizenship restrictions were aimed at reducing the Asian and Muslim populations of Australia to insignificant numbers. To achieve this, the *Immigration Restriction Act* constructed categories whereby Syrians (or Lebanese), for example, were classified as 'Asians'. While they passed the eligibility test for immigration, they were nevertheless excluded from applying for Australian citizenship.[4] However, the racial vilification and internment of enemy migrants during World War I saw Lebanese and Syrians categorised as 'Turkish subjects' and, thus, they were singled out as disloyal and a potential risk to Australian society. It is a disquieting element of Australian history that racial discrimination was openly practised against Muslims, Arabs and Asians—indeed, all migrants of non-Anglo-European stock—under the pretext of cultural homogeneity, social cohesion and the 'national interest'.[5] This was exemplified by the White Australia Policy's infamous dictation test, which was applied with the specific purpose of weeding out the most unfavourable people of the time, as the Secretary of the Department of External Affairs explained to Prime Minister Barton in 1902:

> We continue to eject the monstrous Jap and the wily Chow with persistence. The I.R. [Immigration Restriction] Act has not exhausted its possibilities yet. I have four matters now with the A-G [Attorney-General] for opinion. The April returns show that no coloured aliens passed the test, over 40 were rejected, mostly Chows who tried to enter Queensland on false papers.[6]

It was not until after World War II, almost half a century later, that migration policy started to expand beyond the tight constraints of white Anglo- and Euro-centrism, and Muslims, mostly Turks, started migrating to Australia. With Australia's gradual adoption of a more flexible multicultural policy, the Muslim population has slowly increased; however, widespread ignorance of the cultural and religious diversity of some migrant groups has lingered on. For instance, most Lebanese migrants to Australia prior to 1975 were Christian, and it was only after the outbreak of civil war in Lebanon in 1975 that much greater numbers of Lebanese arrivals were Muslim. Muslims now represent almost 40 per cent of the Lebanese-born population in Australia[7], and of Muslims living in Australia but born overseas the majority are from Lebanon (10 per cent) and Turkey (8.3 per cent). Muslims settling in Australia in more recent times also come from Afghanistan, Iraq and Palestine due to events in their homelands, but also on the increase are North Africans, some of whom identify themselves as Arab Muslims.[8] Although the number of 'onshore' asylum seekers arriving in Australia has fallen, the majority reaching Australia in recent years has been Muslims from Afghanistan, and Muslims and Christians from Iraq.[9] While over three-quarters of Muslims in Australia speak English, 86.5 per cent speak a language other than English at home. The largest percentage of this group is of Arabic-speaking background (94 200), twice as many as those who speak Turkish (45 930).[10] Australian Muslims live mainly in the metropolitan centres of Sydney and Melbourne, and the majority are working class.[11]

In 2001, there were around 282 000 Muslims living in Australia, comprising 1.5 per cent of the population.[12] This had increased by almost 21 per cent by 2006, when the Census recorded just over 340 000 Muslims. This continues to reflect a significant religious minority, comprising only 1.7 per cent of the population, and also represents a smaller increase than, say, the number of Hindus in Australia, which doubled from 2001 to 2006 with a 55.1 per cent increase.[13] As in the 2001 Census, around 36 per cent of Australian Muslims were born in Australia.[14] In 2006, this had increased to 38 per cent, but still with a substantial majority of 62 per cent of Australia's Muslims being born overseas.[15] Of those born in Australia, 85.7 per cent were less than twenty-five years of age in 2001.[16] This makes the Australian Muslim population a very young one at a time when issues of citizenship, identity, representation and loyalty are being heavily scrutinised by politicians, law enforcers and the media due to perceived external security threats. Australians became accustomed to the Howard Government's calls for Muslims to assimilate without delay; however, a change of government in late 2007 has not swept this issue away. In 2008, the new Federal Government was similarly urging Muslims, albeit in a less inflammatory way, to get 'involved in parents groups, sporting clubs [and] political parties'.[17] The Rudd Government's de-emphasis on religious leaders in its newly established Muslim reference group, which is choosing to focus instead on the secular Muslim community,[18] promises to shift the paradigm away from Islam and return issues of assimilation to their rightful place as issues of migrant re-settlement.

Multiculturalism and Citizenship in Australia

During the Howard years, 1996–2007, multiculturalism as an aspiration for national cohesion gradually faded from public discourse and was replaced by a new emphasis on citizenship. The Whitlam-led Labor Government had officially enacted multiculturalism in Australia as policy in 1973. In 2003, three decades later, Prime Minister John Howard would dismiss the very term 'multiculturalism', favouring 'cultural diversity' instead. 'It's [multiculturalism] not a word I use a lot, but there is no other word. I mean I tend to talk about cultural diversity. I tend to talk about people's different heritage.'[19] The policies of the Howard era, which were supported by large sections of the media, did indeed shape public attitudes and views towards Muslim and other migrant communities. This task was made easier by the fact that the Howard Government promoted a version of Australian identity that asserted the dominance of its Anglo-Celtic core[20] with little commitment to a polity that engaged in a meaningful cross-cultural discourse. Howard's Australia and its Anglo-Celtic past had to be embraced by the present because:

> ... whatever we say about our diverse background, the Anglo-Celtic cultural influence is still the most dominant because we speak English and our institutions are, and they were the institutions that attracted a lot of people to this country. We've reached a very comfortable compromise, in a way that I don't think people think our historical antecedents are threatened in any way by this, whereas I do

> think a generation ago some people felt that. Some people
> felt that multiculturalism meant that we had to in some
> way disown our past … [I]t did sort of sound … like that.[21]

This rhetoric appeared to diminish the importance of multiculturalism, or cultural diversity, by situating the past as dominant over the present in its centrality to Australia's cultural identity. In so doing, Australians were encouraged to imagine their futures in much the same way as was encouraged in the days of 'White Australia', that is, establishing criteria through which eligibility for citizenship could be met. Australia thus revived the idea of a test, which was introduced in 2007. It included an understanding of the English language, Australian 'values' and culture, rule of law and democracy. The citizenship test was mooted in September 2006 when a discussion paper 'Australian Citizenship: Much More Than a Ceremony' formally introduced the idea and sought Australians' views. Though several religious organisation submitted policy position papers, including Jewish, Greek Orthodox, Sikh and various Christian denominations, no formal Islamic groups expressed their position on the citizenship test. National associations representing Australians of Egyptian, Malaysian and Pakistani background did, however, contribute and though they were not expressing their views via a religious affiliation, many of their members were representative of Australia's Arab and Muslim communities. While these groups generally support some level of English proficiency before citizenship is granted, the Egyptian and Malaysian-Singaporean submissions, for example, suggested that some values expressed as Australian were really universally held values. The Australian Egyptian Council Forum suggested that it was, indeed, the lack of recognition of these universal values in their original countries that may have caused some migrants to seek a better life in Australia.[22]

Minimising forms of recognition of cultural difference and bracketing identity within a model reminiscent of the 1901 *Immigration Restriction Act* devalues, and even threatens to regress, the evolution of multiculturalism affirmed as central to the Australian notion of a 'fair go' over the last three decades. A return to mere 'tolerance' represents a diminution of the diversity that Australians claim to value highly:

[J]ust 'being tolerated' would not endow the identity they claim with the comforting and healing faculties for which it has been desired. The cognitive frame in which tolerance is granted is totally out of tune with the frame in which it is sought and received … The act of tolerance diminishes, instead of magnifying, the identity's importance.[23]

This is exacerbated by the fact that current economic and political insecurity is generating a more pronounced xenophobic attitude towards migrants in general, and Muslim and Arab Australians in particular. Paradoxically, at a time when strong leadership was needed to correct such attitudes, eleven years of conservative political leadership in Australia tapped into this sense of uncertainty and threat. These paranoid attitudes manifested early on in the Liberal conservative years when in 1996, in her maiden speech, newly elected federal politician Pauline Hanson reintroduced the politics of ethnic divisiveness in Australia.[24] Hanson's right-wing anti-Asian and anti-Aboriginal sentiments resulted in reactionary policies that inhibited the practice of a pluralist, inclusive multiculturalism. Indeed, the term 'multiculturalism' quickly came to represent a threat to a cohesive, Anglo-Australian national identity. This conservative backlash against multiculturalism is a trend now found in many Western nations:

> A second level [of the crisis of modernity] relates to the supposed threat to national culture through imported ethnic cultures. By maintaining their languages, folklore, cultural practices and religions, immigrants are seen as undermining national culture. Racists who attack women in Islamic dress claim to be defending the nation, or even European culture—a stereotype which links up with older racist notions on the threat of the Other to Christianity or civilization.[25]

In September 2006, Prime Minister Howard articulated precisely this anxiety when he singled out Muslims in his call for migrants to learn English, embrace Australian values, and 'fully integrate by treating women as equals', even though he recognised that only a very small section of the Islamic population is resistant to integration.[26] Despite the disclaimer, the Federal Government had repeatedly stereotyped Muslims as an homogenous and problematic group that refused to conform to an acceptable level of 'Australianness'.[27] The range of public responses from the Muslim community to the prime minister's comments—some denouncing and others supporting them[28]—themselves invalidate prevailing assumptions of Islamic homogeneity. One month later, then–parliamentary secretary to the former Minister for Immigration and Multicultural Affairs, Andrew Robb, added to the growing list of expectations of newly arrived migrants by urging them to get a job quickly and to have 'quick and regular interaction with other groups in the community through activities such as sport'.[29] Since then the word 'multicultural', reflecting John Howard's discomfort, has been dropped from the portfolio, which was renamed the Department of Immigration and Citizenship (DIAC) in January 2007. This change echoes a gradual decline in enthusiasm for 'multiculturalism' over the Howard years, and the concurrent rise in emphasis on an implicit commitment to 'citizenship' and its close association with a set of Australian values.

This shift in emphasis in the Howard years from multiculturalism to citizenship and its inherent values is also evident in education policy, and despite the increasingly multi-ethnic nature of Australian society, twenty-first-century education continues to reflect a general uniformity in terms of learning priorities and structures. Education policy in Australia is essentially the preserve of the states; however, the Federal Government maintains a significant interest in steering those areas deemed to be of national concern, such as citizenship, democracy, culture and values. In 1999, *The Adelaide Declaration on National Goals for Schooling in the Twenty-First Century* acknowledged the changing local environment enforced by globalisation, stating that 'This world will be characterised by advances in information and communication technologies, population diversity arising from international mobility and migration, and complex environmental and social challenges.'[30]

The Declaration goes on to specify its key goals, including an understanding and acknowledgement of 'cultural and linguistic diversity[31]', and a commitment to students' school experience being 'free from the effects of negative forms of discrimination based on sex, language, culture and ethnicity, religion or disability'.[32] Since then values have moved to the forefront of federal education policy initiatives with the Values Education Study (2003), the National Report on Schooling in Australia (2003), and a Draft National Framework for Values Education in Australian Schools (2004). These initiatives have worked towards identifying areas where structural change might benefit students, but an acknowledgement of the specific pedagogical and curricular needs of students from multi-ethnic backgrounds has been absent. Indeed, the issue of 'values' in Australia's pluralist cultural setting continues to pose a challenge to policy-makers and educators.

Amid the somewhat elusive definition of precisely what 'Australian values' are, the criteria for 'Australianness' seem to advocate cultural uniformity as the primary 'Australian value', an idea implicit to all but the 'un-Australian other'. Hence, multiculturalism as a concept of national identity, that since the 1970s extended citizenship and belonging to different ethnic groups, seems to have been replaced by a sense of insecurity that calls for the narrower ideal of citizenship, embodying a range of culture-neutral 'values'. In reality, the nation is asked, therefore, to imagine itself as a community that shares the primary common value of citizenship, with its inherent rights and duties grounded by secular legalism, while diverse cultural and religious formations of identity become secondary to that construct. Within this civic nationalist vision, citizenship, as the community bond, presents a challenge for some who may see the difference in the 'other' as divisive and weakening of the social bond and not vice versa.

Muslims and the Media in Australia Post–September 11

Since the attacks on New York in 2001, representations of Muslims in Australia have tended to manifest in two diametrically opposed directions.[33] Either they are virtually ignored by the national media, which effectively denies their membership among the urban citizenry, *or* their activities are represented as inherently disconnected from Australian society, negative and/or violent. This frames them as collectively problematic and potentially a source of security threat to the nation. It could be argued that this duality has traditionally applied to ethnic groups in Australia more broadly, and hence many Australians simultaneously take pride in the culturally diverse nature of their society while historically giving political support to narrow conservative policy approaches to multiculturalism and nationalist identity politics. Several examples since September 11 can be cited in which negative assumptions have come to dominate public perceptions of Muslims in Australia. First is the punitive stance towards asylum seekers arriving in Australia, who in the last decade have increasingly been of Arab and/or Muslim origin. Though the plight of Indochinese 'boat people' in the late 1970s was viewed with some sympathy, the public attitude has shifted towards greater 'desensitisation' on refugee issues since the 1980s. In particular during the Howard years, the Australian public largely supported a harsher approach. This was aggravated by the ambiguous and sometimes difficult intersection of the increasingly complex and fluid notions of identity, nationalism and multiculturalism which can easily move from exclusionary discourse to immigration policy. However, recent dissent in Federal Parliament against the position on refugees and detention from within the conservative Liberal Party itself, but also from the new Labor Government, has started to water down, and in some cases dismantle, some of the more punitive policies such as mandatory detention of children and temporary protection visas.

In the case of the harsh treatment of asylum seekers, some have argued that the globalised politics of neo-capitalism is essentially responsible for eroding society's capacity to generate care for others and distribute hope for a better future.[34] This is because states have become 'managers' of national economies to the detriment of the wellbeing of their citizenry, whose sense of economic vulnerability results in negative nationalist discourses framed within the language of worry, insecurity and defensive border policing. This worrying insecurity about oneself and the nation then manifests as a form of paranoia and indifference to the suffering of those excluded from the national imaginary on the basis of their cultural traits. Ghassan Hage locates the current mood of worry over the form that the national identity is taking in the shift from the descriptive multiculturalism of the 1970s, which was 'perceived primarily as a form of welfare and of cultural government', to today's multiculturalism 'that is more pre-scriptive and perceived to be primarily about national identity'.[35] This latter approach to multiculturalism, he argues, marks a return to the fragility of colonial identity and its anxieties about a loss of the

Anglo-Celtic self a century ago and, hence, the narrower parameters drawn around citizenship and belonging as discussed earlier.

Another instance of the use of race to discredit an entire community and culture was that of a rape case involving Lebanese youth in Sydney where, this time, negative assumptions overrode the impartiality implicit in secular law. Coinciding with the September 2001 attacks on New York, the trial of this case marked a point at which Muslims—and Muslim men in particular—were stigmatised as a public threat. In August 2000, a group of young Lebanese men gang raped four young women in Sydney, and two years later, in August 2002, one of the men involved was given a record sentence of fifty-five years with a minimum of forty years without parole. Two others received considerable jail terms of twenty-three and eighteen years respectively. Debates in the media raged over whether the rapes were racially motivated or ethnically linked. 'The rapists, Muslim Lebanese-Australians, had apparently told their victims that they were targeting "Aussie pigs"'.[36]

The then–Premier of New South Wales, Bob Carr, established himself as a commentator on this particular trial, asking Lebanese-Australian parents to 'take control of your boys'.[37] Carr was criticised for his contribution to the media's portrayal of the rapes as ethnic crimes associated with the culture of the entire Sydney Lebanese Muslim community. Hage commented that Carr had invited 'everyone in the State to make a public link between "Lebanese", "gangs" and "rapists"', and Hanifa Deen added that 'The public and the politicians lay the blame at the door of Lebanese parents and the "un-Australian" culture they brought with them.'[38] Some media commentators, such as Janet Albrechtsen in *The Australian*, tried to establish an intrinsic link between the crime and the ethnicity of the offenders. In September 2001, she argued that there was a direct link between Islamic culture in Western societies and the gang rape of white girls, going on to suggest that Muslim youth were caught up in an inherent conflict between the Islamic values of their parents and the liberal values promoted by Western societies.[39] New South Wales Anti-Discrimination Board president, Chris Puplick, called the media reports of the rapes racist, linking them to other instances of the media's intolerance towards Australians of Middle Eastern background since September 11.[40] The NSW Premier, however, defended the reportage, arguing that the offenders themselves introduced the issue of ethnicity into the crimes. He also defended the use of ethnic descriptors such as 'of Middle Eastern appearance' in crime reporting, arguing that the 'description of a suspect's ethnicity [will] enhance the prospects of success[41]' in solving crimes. One has to question the insinuation that ethnic descriptors are a neutral tool for helping to locate offenders of crime, because their use perpetuates racial stereotypes, which can in turn implicate whole communities. 'One suspects these descriptors also helped vigilantes in the community in their witch hunt. Being described as short, tall, dark haired or blonde is vastly different to being portrayed as 'of Middle Eastern appearance'—the latter is pejorative in today's climate, as well as being imprecise.'[42]

A third instance of blatant stigmatisation came about, somewhat ironically, during anti-war protests on 26 March 2003, which generated more negative media reports about Arab and Muslim Australians, whose mere participation attracted hostility. Shortly after the war in Iraq had begun, a national student anti-war organisation, Books Not Bombs, held a peace march in Sydney's central business district. The peace protest received significant media coverage around Australia; with much of the corporate media claiming that young men 'of Middle Eastern appearance' had 'hijacked' the protest and incited violence against the police. Footage of the mayhem was shown, and the press, such as Sydney's highest circulation tabloid, the *Daily Telegraph*, reported:

> With bottles and knives in their hands and hate in their hearts, a mob of violent troublemakers yesterday ambushed a student anti-war rally to lead a vicious rampage through Sydney streets. A group of young men, described by police as 'Middle Eastern males' created havoc by throwing chairs, rocks, bottles, eggs and golf balls at the police and media during several hours of chaos in the CBD.[43]

Further reports revealed, however, that in fact the conflict on the day was initiated by police actions targeting young Arab-Australians. At the outset, police forcefully arrested two males in their early teens, beating back the crowd in the process. One officer tore a hijab scarf from the head of a young Muslim woman and pushed her, antagonising the crowd which erupted, throwing chairs in anger. The crowd later congregated in Hyde Park to listen to speakers, during which a 14-year-old Muslim girl was arrested, sparking a further angry response. It was reported that police continued to use provocative tactics, at one point trapping the crowd against the side of a building.[44]

In the ensuing media condemnation of the protesters, particularly the 'Middle Eastern youth', talkback hosts on Sydney radio gave out the telephone number and address of the organising centre of Books Not Bombs. Key figures in the organisation subsequently received death threats. At further protests, young Arab-Australian men and boys were singled out by journalists and asked 'Are you here for a fight?'[45] Responses to the protest received by the *Daily Telegraph* were indicative of the severity of the slippage between notions of Arab culture, Muslim culture, violence, conflict and terrorism that has appeared in some sections of public discourse. The level of fear and distrust of the Arab-Australian community was revealed in one comment: 'If the Middle Eastern men who attacked the police yesterday are an example of what happens to a community when you accept Arab Islamic asylum seekers or immigrants then I hope the country doesn't make the mistake again.'[46]

The Media and the Problematising of Gender in Islam

The stereotyping of gender in Islam, where males are depicted as defiant and militant and females as passive and repressed, has been perpetuated by the media's propensity to assert simple solutions to complex problems and, of course, its tendency towards sensationalism. While this became acute during the rape case discussed, as well as post–September 11, it is a phenomenon that pre-dates the rise of terrorism. In the late 1990s, a 'moral panic about "Lebanese youth gangs"' was triggered after a drive-by shooting in Sydney's Lakemba. Reported in the *Daily Telegraph* as 'An Act of War[47]', this was perhaps the defining moment when young men of Middle Eastern background were branded as a group alienated from Australian 'values'. Exacerbated by the rape case and the New York terrorist attacks, mistrust of even the most assimilated first, second and third generation Australians of Arab or Islamic background deepened.

Paradoxically, however, when mistrust and stigmatisation are generated by narrow media essentialism, young people are at risk of moving closer towards a 'cliquish mentality[48]' in order to reinforce their sense of identity and belonging. This tendency has been demonstrated in articles written by prominent Muslims, such as Dr Zachariah Matthews and Siddiq Buckley, in their calls for Australian Muslims of all cultural and ethnic backgrounds to unite in a solidarity defined by their faith.[49] Exclusionary and divisive attitudes, therefore, tend to result in more defensive minority communities appealing to each other to 'stick together' against a society that defines people of a particular cultural or religious group as 'guilty until proven innocent'.[50] This form of social bonding is often practised among members of minority groups and communities as a result of feelings of exclusion, alienation or threat. The culmination of this series of events, and a consequent deepening of mistrust in some parts of Sydney in particular, culminated in Cronulla in December 2005.

In the reporting of the rape case and the riots in particular, the media rather too effortlessly reinscribed 'social problems as racial problems[51]', further entrenching the idea of social dysfunction within ethnic communities which, in this case, was intensified by perceptions of Islamic misogyny. The Cronulla riots represented an eruption of tensions that had been building for some time, largely in relation to Muslim responses to Australian girls wearing bikinis on the beach. Perceptions on each side of moral righteousness around 'how we treat our women' served also to distance the dominant culture and mitigate any broader sense of social responsibility. The response to the riots, it could be argued, over-determined what was deemed 'racial conflict', throwing up fears of a subliminal 'White Australia' national mentality, rather than reporting the riots as an isolated incident of intercultural conflict. In contemplating the exposure of Australians' anxiety about its racist inclinations after the Cronulla riots, David Burchell agreed with Hage's argument that multiculturalism implies that a 'core', culturally privileged majority (that is, Anglo-Celtic) extends its beneficent toleration to a 'periphery' of disadvantaged minority cultural, religious and ethnic groups (everyone else). However, the dominant core is itself impoverished by a 'cultural and ethnic statelessness', that is, a deficiency in its own defining cultural, often religious, and ethnic richness, and depends upon the periphery to fill this void. This provides 'no vantage point from which disputes between members of "peripheral" groups and members of the core can be understood, except through the prism of cultural domination'.[52]

The Cronulla riots, unlike Lebanese–Vietnamese tensions in places like Sydney's Lakemba or Cabramatta, were characterised as a territorial confrontation between culturally rigid Middle Eastern males and the quintessentially easygoing 'Aussie' surfer. Rioters from the 'periphery'—the Middle Eastern—were characteristically cast as 'frustrated and marginalised'. Rioters from the Anglo-Celtic 'core', however, presented a much more profound concern in that a deep-seated national racist character that still lurks within the Australian psyche was exposed:

> It's often true that when young men of marginal social or economic status riot, they're expressing some wider distress which their fellow-citizens, and policy-makers, ought to take seriously. But the framework through which 'progressive' folks mostly interpreted the Cronulla riots and their aftermath mostly works to preclude such concerns. The surfer-boys' concern that 'their' beaches had been taken over by outsiders, that the public space of the area had been made less safe, and their girlfriends' sunbaking less secure, are no doubt overblown.[53]

Burchell goes on to conclude that it is most likely that both the Lebanese boys and Aussie surfer-boys come from a 'suburban youth culture revolving around creative idleness and illegal employment' and that their socio-economic backgrounds are 'probably rather similar'.[54] Localised intercommunal tension, sparked by mutual suspicions of the 'other', further aroused national anxiety about racism, a socio-cultural position deemed to be the province of the dominant 'us'. But as Hage was at pains to explain on the ABC's *Four Corners* in its investigation of the Lebanese gang-rape case:

> There is no doubt that before the sentencing there's been enough media coverage which has tried to portray what's been happening as a white Anglo-Australian civilised

> Australian versus uncivilised Muslim Lebanese people. … I
> mean like why can't there be racist Lebanese? I mean what
> is it that makes Lebanese supposed to be angels? … So
> what? There are Lebanese racists. Why should the Lebanese
> be different from anyone, you know?[55]

This tendency to ascribe 'racism' as a privilege of the dominant culture is itself revealing. As Hage's comment suggests, minority immigrant groups are expected to have renounced access to any sense of equality when settling in Australia, and it remains at the discretion of the majority culture as to when, and whether, equality will be extended. This right can be assumed by anyone, from institutional elites down to the humble 'Aussie surfer', by virtue of membership of the dominant culture. But members of a minority ethnic, religious or racial group, have no such access and, therefore, no rights of disapproval over the activities of the dominant group. It is also revealing that, in an era when 'race' as a scientific fact—which legitimised 'white' superiority from the nineteenth to mid-twentieth centuries—has been debunked as a biological reality, that the term retains its currency. *Critical Race Theory: An Introduction* defines racism as 'Any program or practice of discrimination, segregation, persecution or mistreatment based on membership in a race or ethnic group.'[56] So, although 'race' as a concept no longer has any credibility, the term 'racism' remains in circulation by virtue of the importance placed upon social *membership*. The Lebanese rape case and the Cronulla riots were particularly telling moments for Australia in this respect. First, these events exposed a readiness to disavow crime and pose it as an 'imported problem' as suggested by New South Wales Premier Bob Carr.[57] Similarly, the misogyny that resulted in gang rape was portrayed as a dysfunction of Islam, although as Pat O'Shane pointed out, 'Indigenous Australian women have been subjected to such criminal behaviour by Anglo-Australian men … without a single bleat from the likes of [Janet] Albrechtsen [from *The Australian*].'[58]

For young Australian Muslims, mostly of Lebanese descent, the effect has been particularly damaging, forcing boys to keep a low profile, especially in Sydney, at the time of the gang-rape case. High-profile Muslim sportsmen and role models for Arab and Muslim Australian youth, such as soccer player Ahmed Elrich and boxer Hussein Hussein, kept their public presence to a minimum at the time and reported feeling uncomfortable speaking with women. As Hussein commented, 'We are all on trial.'[59] It would be unthinkable for a rape trial of a group of Anglo-Australian men to cast all Anglo-Australian males with the suspicion of sexual deviousness.

The reporting of this series of incidents revealed the media's role in agitating suspicions that Arab and Muslim men are violent and unpredictable, while Muslim women are sexually oppressed, powerless victims of male aggression. In August 2006, *The Australian* newspaper announced 'Children exported as brides', a front-page story claiming that 'Australian girls as young as 14 have been flown overseas and forced to marry older men in an attempt by their families to protect them from promiscuity and Western influences at home.'[60]

Again, it was Lebanese Muslims who were under scrutiny. It was not the truth of the article that was as concerning as the application of such reports to an entire community rather than to the very small section of Australian Muslim society to which it relates. Furthermore, contrary to *The Australian*'s feature article 'Brides of Islam', published on the same day, a large section of Lebanese society that might adhere to arranged marriage is Christian. Arranged marriage, as indicated by Muslim leaders[61], is a cultural practice, rather than an Islamic one. Indeed, it is widely known that Indian culture, for example, favours arranged marriage and this custom is often practised in Indian Diasporic communities drawing little attention from the media. More critical to some parents of Muslim background in Australia are their concerns about differences in, and a perceived lack of, morality in Australia. In this respect, similar to Burchell's framing of a 'cultural and ethnic statelessness', is a 'moral statelessness' whereby the moral guidelines formerly inscribed by religion are more difficult to discern in a society which is increasingly less inclined towards religious affiliation.[62] 'Australian values' as advocated by the Federal Government are rather nebulous or, at the very least, difficult to discern as distinctly 'Australian', as they represent the broad rules of citizenship, primarily adherence to democracy and to the rule of law. This set of values, devised by the secular state, is applicable to the public domain, and private morality in Australia remains the province of the individual. Except if you are a Muslim. The Federal Government has stated unequivocally that if Muslims want to practise sharia law, they should 'clear off[63]'; however, sharia is rather more complex in that it informs both the public and private realms of Islamic life. In the absence of this understanding of Islam, Muslims' private morality is scrutinised, yet the right of non-Muslims to live by their own private moral precepts, whatever they might be, remains sacrosanct.

Muslims and the Politics of Race and Insecurity

The instances of Muslim stereotyping through the media illustrates the degree to which the media is free to shape, distort or expose (mis)representations of any particular social group. This is a particularly potent liberty in circumstances of insecurity, such as current concerns over international terrorism, when there is an urge to forge a strong national identity through the construction of an enemy. This time, it is the Muslims casting a shadow across both international and national security and stability, despite the fact that terrorism is not, and has never been, the preserve of Muslims alone. September 11 invoked a considerable backlash against Arab and Muslim Australians for a number of reasons.[64] Suffice to say that the nature of the act itself sparked outrage, horror and intense shock throughout the world. Understandably the Western world, and in particular the United States, felt the impact of the tragedy profoundly as, despite the fact that spasmodic terrorist acts had been initiated against US interests, none of this magnitude had ever been orchestrated and directed at American civilians. There was incomprehension in the West as to why an event like this would occur in America. The need to reconcile what seemed irreconcilable saw blame crystallising on Osama bin Laden, and by association Islam itself, which he claimed to represent. September 11 followed a series of terrorist activities over a number of decades through which Islam had been portrayed as a threat to the 'free world'. This event cemented some Western leaders', and the Western mass media's, positioning of Islam as a homogeneous entity that incites primordial anti-Western violence: 'Perhaps more clearly than through any event in the past, Islam was seen as providing a rationale for mass murder and terrorism, emphasised by bin Laden's rhetoric'.[65]

The Western media and other sources of anti-Islamic discourse pointed to bin Laden's anti-Western statements and the expressions of joy on the streets of Palestine at the events as evidence that Islam was a bloodthirsty, primitive religion that promoted terrorist activities.[66] Moreover, the element of surprise caused instant insecurity and paranoia throughout the Western world, which previously had been complacent in its shelter from violent conflict within its domestic borders. Compounded by the fact that some of the September 11 terrorists had operated in the United States through migration networks, panicked sections of the public in Western nations who—prompted by some media outlets and conservative governments—looked at their fellow citizens, and also at asylum seekers, whether Arab, Muslim or both, as followers of a violent, incompatible religion, potential terrorists and untrustworthy individuals.[67] Events closer to home—the Bali bombings in October 2002 and the bombing of the Australian Embassy in Jakarta in 2004, both of which were linked with Jemaah Islamiyah, and by association to Al-Qaeda—reinforced Australian anxieties that terrorism was a domestic potentiality. The arrests in November 2005 of a 'terror cell' of nine in Melbourne and seven in Sydney, the alleged leader of which was a Muslim cleric, and a further three arrests in Melbourne in April 2006, have affirmed the notion of jihad as a domestic plausibility in Australia. The majority of those arrested were young men in their twenties who, like the young British-born Pakistani suicide bombers who carried out the attacks on the London Underground in July 2005, seemed to have merged unobtrusively into their adopted country. The shock of the perpetrators' proximity and their lack of patriotism deepened scepticism towards Muslims as a disloyal, devious and deceitful group, particularly where young men are concerned.

This deep suspicion of Islam transcends nationality, as demonstrated in the case of 'Jihad' Jack Thomas, a 33-year-old fifth-generation Australian who converted to Islam and spent time in Afghanistan and Pakistan with his Indonesian wife. The courts found Jack Thomas not guilty of the terrorism convictions against him in his first trial, prompting outrage from some sections of Australian society and the media. Jack Thomas's retrial began in April 2007, was adjourned until September 2007, and has consistently been referred to in the media as a 'terror trial'. This perceived mistrust of the Australian courts to correctly apply the law to Jack Thomas or to report it in a tone of impartiality implicit in the Australian legal system, implies that it is his allegiance to Islam, more than his alleged terrorist activities, that remains in the dock. This seems particularly ironic given the centrality of the rule of law as an 'Australian value', an understanding of which forms an intrinsic part of the rights and duties of citizenship. Jack Thomas' case returned to the courts—and to the media—in June 2008 with his appeal to the High Court to stop a retrial going ahead. That appeal was lost and the trial, based on statements made in an interview Thomas gave to the ABC's *Four Corners* program, went ahead. The nature of Jack Thomas' ongoing trial was evidence of the significant degree to which the media is not only fervently interested in, but has become heavily embroiled in, the issue of Australia's nascent anti-terrorism legislation. Similar to the Mohammed Haneef case, so-called 'terror trials' have become media events that, in satiating a perceived public desire for evidence of an Islamic threat, potentially inflame rather than quell fears of the Muslim 'other'. However, in both instances, the cases have not been successfully sustained.

A paradigm shift in the last decade in Australia has occurred on a range of levels. First, the move away from 'multiculturalism' towards the more homogenised notion of citizenship, as expressed in the Department of Immigration's recent name change, has gradually institutionalised a diminishing sense of cultural inclusiveness in Australia. Second, the rise of Australian 'values', despite a prevailing sense of nebulousness as to precisely what they are, has gradually made its way into policy, perhaps most influentially in education policy. Third, there has been an increase in media stereotyping, with its edge of demonisation of Muslims since September 2001, and calls for them to assimilate quickly. We begin to see how the shift towards intolerance of Islam in the West has the potential to adversely impact upon the young at a critical time of identity formation. The recognition of these psychological shifts in Australia's attitude towards its diverse cultural composition, and how it has manoeuvred the Muslim community into a paradoxical social position—where belonging is both encouraged and discouraged—motivated the *Diversity Project* to take up its work in secondary schools. The following chapter explores the lived experience of Arab and Muslim youth in Australia within the theoretical framework of 'multicultural education' and analyses how this framework applies within culturally diverse educational settings in Australia.

Notes

1   It is, in fact, argued, though not yet firmly established, that Muslims
     came to the north of Australia via the Indonesian archipelago as early as
     the 13th century, well before Christians. See B. Cleland, *A History of
     Islam in Australia*, Islam for Today, www.islamfortoday.com/australia03.
     htm, viewed 18 March 2008.
2   C Stevens, 1989, *Tin Mosques & Ghantowns: A History of Afghan Camel
     Drivers in Australia*, Oxford University Press, Melbourne. See especially
     Chapter Five, 'Conflict', pp. 139–66.
3   Trevor Batrouney, 2002, 'From "White Australia" to Multiculturalism:
     Citizenship and Identity', in Ghassan Hage (ed.), *Arab-Australians Today:
     Citizenship and Belonging*, Melbourne University Press, Melbourne,
     pp. 37–62; see also Fethi Mansouri, 2005, 'Citizenship, Identity and
     Belonging in Contemporary Australia', in S Akbarzadeh and S Yasmeen
     (eds), *Islam and the West: Reflections from Australia*, UNSW Press,
     Sydney, pp. 114–32.
4   Andrew Batrouney, 2003, 'Arabic Immigration to Australia', paper
     presented at the conference 'Arabic Smoke Free Sunday', Melbourne,
     18 August, p. 8.
5   It is important to note that these exclusionary practices were not
     peculiar to Australia. America, and the settler societies of Canada and
     New Zealand, developed similar policies designed to preserve their
     Anglo-Celtic heritage.
6   From a letter written by the Secretary of the Department of External
     Affairs, Atlee Hunt, to the Prime Minister, Edmund Barton, 28 May, 1902,
     Barton Papers, MS 51/1/976, National Library of Australia, Canberra.
7   Trevor Batrouney, p. 40.
8   Wafia Omar and Kirsty Allen, 1997, *The Muslims in Australia*, Australian
     Government Printing Service, Canberra, p. 10.
9   For example, more than 9500 people, mainly from Afghanistan and Iraq,
     arrived in Australia unlawfully by boat between July 1999 and December
     2001. Department of Immigration and Citizenship 2007, *Fact Sheet 75:
     Processing Unlawful Boat Arrivals. Australian Government*, DIAC, www.
     immi.gov.au/media/fact-sheets/75processing.htm, viewed 18 June 2007.
10   ibid., p. 1, quoting 2001 census figures (281,590 Muslims in Australia in
     2001).
11   ibid., p. 2.
12   A Saeed, 2003, *Islam in Australia*, Allen & Unwin, Sydney, p. 1. This figure
     relies on the 2001 Census. At the time of writing, data from the 2006
     Census, completed by Australians on 8 August, had not been collated.
13   Australian Bureau of Statistics, *Year Book Australia, 2008*, www.abs.gov.
     au/AUSSTATS, viewed 1 April 2008.
14   Department of Immigration and Citizenship, 2007, 'Muslims in Australia
     – A Snapshot'. See www.immi.gov.au/living-in-australia/a-diverse-
     australia/communities/muslim-community/conference-Australian_
     Imams/Muslims_in_Australia_snapshot.pdf, viewed 18 June 2007.
15   Australian Bureau of Statistics, *Year Book Australia, 2008*.

16   ibid.
17   R Kerbaj 2008, 'Rudd's Request for True Blue Muslims', *The Australian*,
      11 March.
18   ibid.
19   G Megalogenis, 2002, 'Multicultural Australia Examined: The Full-Text
      of the John Howard Interview', *The Australian*, 6 February,
      www.theaustralian.news.com.au/common/story_page/0,5744,4264645%
      255E21207,00.html; see also David Hollinsworth, 1998, *Race and Racism
      in Australia*, Social Science Press, Sydney, pp. 269–76.
20   See Hollinsworth; see also Ghassan Hage quoted in Hollinsworth, p. 274.
21   John Howard quoted in Megalogenis.
22   See the Department of Immigration and Citizenship website for more
      detail about the citizenship test and the community submissions made.
      The *Summary Report on the Outcomes of the Public Consultation on the
      Merits of Introducing a Formal Citizenship Test* can be found at
      www.minister.immi.gov.au/media/responses/citizenship-test/
      insdex.htm, viewed 20 April 2007.
23   Z Bauman, 2001, 'The Great War of Recognition', *Theory, Culture
      and Society*, vol. 18, nos 2–3, p. 144.
24   For an account of Pauline Hanson's impact on Australian politics see
      Michael Leach, Geoffrey Stokes and Ian Ward (eds), 2000, *The Rise and
      Fall of One Nation*, University of Queensland Press, St Lucia.
25   Stephen Castles, 1996, 'The Racisms of Globalization', in Ellie Vasta and
      Stephen Castles (eds), *The Teeth are Smiling*, Allen & Unwin, NSW, p. 40.
26   Richard Kerbaj, 2006, 'PM Tells Muslims to Learn English',
      The Australian, 1 September, p. 1.
27   Note Howard's, Costello's and Ruddock's media statements on this,
      see endnote 49 in this chapter.
28   Mustapha Kara-Ali, youth representative of the Muslim Community
      Reference Group, agreed with Mr Howard's comments that Muslims
      should learn English, while Dr Ameer Ali, head of the Government's
      Muslim Advisory Committee, warned Mr Howard's comments could
      lead to more Cronulla riots. See Luke McIlvean, 2006, 'Young Muslim
      Leader Backs Howard' *Daily Telegraph*, 5 September; and 'Muslims Warn
      of Cronulla-Style Riots' 2006, *The Age*, 1 September, respectively. It is
      interesting to note that Mr Kara-Ali's moderate comments were
      attributed in the headline to himself alone, while Dr Ali's more
      reactionary response was attributed to 'Muslims' generally.
29   Andrew Robb, 2006, 'Opening Address' at the 'Adult Migrant English
      Program National Conference – Cultures of Learning', Perth, 5 October,
      www.minister.immi.gov.au/parlsec/media/speeches/cultures_learning.
      htm, viewed 6 November 2006.
30   'The Adelaide Declaration on National Goals for Schooling in the
      Twenty-first Century' was developed at the 10th Ministerial Council on
      Education, Employment, Training and Youth Affairs (MCEETYA) in
      Adelaide, 22–23 April 1999 by State, Territory and Federal Government
      Ministers. See www.dest.gov.au/schools/adelaide/adelaide.htm.

31   ibid., Goal 3.5.

32   ibid., Goal 3.1.

33   KM Dunn, 1998, 'Rethinking Ethnic Concentration: Cabramatta,
      The Case of Sydney', *Urban Studies*, vol. 35, no. 3, pp. 503–27, 515.

34   Ghassan Hage, 2003, *Against Paranoid Nationalism: Searching for Hope
      in a Shrinking Society*, Pluto Press, Australia.

35   ibid., p. 60.

36   CNN World, 2002, 'Record Rape Sentence Rocks Australia', *CNN.com
      World*, 16 August, www.cnn.com/2002/WORLD/asiapcf/auspac/08/16/
      australia.legal/, viewed 18 June 2007.

37   H Deen, 2003, *Caravanserai: Journey Among Australian Muslims*,
      Fremantle Arts Centre Press, Fremantle, pp. 271–9, 303.

38   Hage, *Against Paranoid Nationalism*, p. 242; see also ibid., p. 302.

39   Deen, pp. 304–5.

40   *The Australian*, 2003, 'Gang Rape Reports not Racist: Carr', 12 March,
      www.theaustralian.news.com.au/printpage/0,5942,6162179,00.html,
      viewed 30 July 2003.

41   Carr quoted in Deen, p. 307.

42   ibid., p. 307.

43   Emma Clancy, 2003, 'Carr Government Bans Student Peace March',
      Green Left Weekly, 2 April.

44   ibid.

45   Emma Clancy, 2003, 'Sorry to Disappoint the Media', *Green Left Weekly*,
      9 April.

46   *The Daily Telegraph*, 2003, 'General Comments on War Issues', 27 March.

47   Greg Noble and Scott Poynting, 2003, 'Acts of War: Military Metaphors in
      Representations of Lebanese Youth Gangs', *Media International
      Australia incorporating Culture and Policy*, no. 106, February, p. 110.

48   Ghassan Hage in interview with Stephen McDonell, 2002, 'Interview
      with Dr Ghassan Hage', *Four Corners*, Australian Broadcasting
      Corporation, 26 August, www.abc.net.au/4corners/stories/s677558.htm,
      viewed 30 May 2006.

49   See Dr Zachariah Matthews' article 'Unity in the Face of Adversity' from
      his address at the launch of the Islamic Legal Fund on 2 July 2004;
      see also Siddiq Buckley's 'Australian Muslims: Alert and Alarmed!', in
      Salam Magazine's Guilty of Being Muslim issue, 26 November 2005 on
      the FAMSY (Federation of Australian Muslims and Youth) website.

50   ibid.

51   Noble and Poynting, 'Acts of War', p. 113.

52   David Burchell, 2006, 'An Email from the Ether: After the Cronulla
      Events', *Australian Universities Review*, vol. 48, no. 2, p. 7.

53   ibid., p. 8.

54   ibid.

55   Hage interview with McDonnell.

56   Richard Delgado and Jean Stefancic, 2001, *Critical Race Theory:
      An Introduction*, New York University Press, New York and London, p. 154.

57   Noble and Poynting, 'Acts of War', p. 114.

58   Scott Poynting, Greg Noble, Paul Tabar and Jock Collins, 2004, *Bin Laden
      in the Suburbs: Criminalising the Arab Other*, Sydney Institute of
      Criminology Series, p. 144.
59   Hussein quoted in Nadia Jamal and Taghred Chandah, 2005, *The Glory
      Garage: Growing up Lebanese Muslim in Australia*, Allen & Unwin,
      Sydney, p. 116.
60   Trudy Harris, 2005, 'Children Exported as Brides', *The Australian*,
      2 August.
61   ibid.
62   'The proportion of all Australians stating an affiliation to some type of
      religion remained relatively stable from 1933 until 1971, at slightly less
      than 90%. This proportion dropped to 80% in 1976, then slowly declined
      to 73% in 2001. This gradual fall occurred against a backdrop of change
      in social values and attitudes, particularly since the late 1960s, and an
      increased secularisation of society in the last three decades of the 20th
      century. It was accompanied by a rising tendency among all Australians
      to state that they did not affiliate with any religion, particularly evident
      since the 1970s (7% in 1971 and 16% in 2001).' This trend was
      accompanied by an increase in affiliations with Hinduism, Buddhism
      and Islam, reflecting changes in the countries of origin of migrants.
      Excerpt from *Australian Social Trends 2004*, Australian Bureau of
      Statistics, www.abs.gov.au, last updated 28 April 2006, viewed 15 August
      2006.
63   There has been much media attention given to this issue in 2005 and
      2006. See, for example, Michelle Grattan, 2005, 'Accept Australian Values
      or Get Out', *The Age*, 25 August; and Josh Gordon and Jewel Tospfield,
      2006, 'Our Values or Go Home: Costello', *The Age*, 24 February.
64   See, for example, Noam Chomsky's two short books *September 11*, Allen
      & Unwin, USA and Australia, 2001; and *Power and Terror: Post-9/11 Talks
      and Interviews*, Seven Stories Press, New York, 2003, for more discussion
      on this.
65   Saeed, *Islam in Australia*, p. 186.
66   Ghassan Hage, 2002, 'Postscript: Arab-Australian Belonging After
      "September 11"', in Ghassan Hage (ed.), *Arab-Australians Today*,
      pp. 241–8, 243.
67   ibid., p. 243.

CHAPTER 2

The Social and Educational Experiences of Arab and Muslim Australian Youth

In this chapter the schooling experiences of migrant youth in Australia and the impact of education upon identity formation are first examined in general terms. We then, more specifically, apply these dynamics to the experiences of Arab and Muslim youth, and look at a range of studies involving these groups that have been undertaken in Australia since the 1990s. By way of foregrounding the social and educational experiences of Arab and Muslim youth, however, we first look to some of the theoretical approaches adopted for conceptualising culture, cultural diversity and cultural identity among youth. We examine how first- and second-generation migrant youth negotiate cultural identity in the private spaces of family networks and in the public sphere where ethnic, gendered and racial perceptions interact to shape social and behavioural outcomes. We then examine extant studies into migrant youth in Australia to more specifically position Arab and Muslim Australian youth within this discourse.

Theoretical approaches to culture have been conceptualised through a range of disciplines and perspectives. Indeed, the concept of culture has become 'a contested domain[1]' that has been 'examined, poked at, pushed, rolled over, killed, revived, and reified ad infinitum[2]' to the point where it is difficult to pin down. When the first anthropological definition of culture was introduced by Edward Tylor in 1871, it was equated with 'civilisation, taken in its widest ethnographic sense', constituting the 'complex whole which includes knowledge, belief, arts, morals, law, customs, and any other capabilities and habits acquired by man as a member of society'.[3] Little wonder, then, that this broad concept has inspired heated academic debate and interdisciplinary contest over successive generations about 'the methods, evidence and goals of scholarly research'.[4] Rather than taking a disciplinary approach, therefore, it is perhaps more useful to view culture through the prisms of social interactivity.

Most of the literature on first- and second-generation migrants and their children positions culture within a 'centre-periphery relationship[5]', or the competing paradigms of majority culture versus minority culture(s), and attendant processes of social and cultural inclusion or exclusion. However, the fundamental problem with this conceptual framework is that it is far easier to ascribe 'ethnocratic' labels to cultures (for example, Australian culture, Vietnamese-Australian culture or Arab youth culture) than it is to identify what such labels mean in practical terms.[6] Ethno-cultural labels assume a high level of cultural homogeneity within a given ethnic group without accounting for areas of cultural overlap in migrant communities, which themselves may be multicultural.[7] They also often fail to consider variances in socio-economic status, religion, gender[8], race or proficiency in the host culture's language[9], which in turn determine the capacity of first- and second-generation migrants to access institutional resources to try and make their cultural definition 'stick' and prevent others' definitions from being heard.[10] That is, 'categorisation and hierarchisation are undoubtedly methods for the distribution' of cultural values and norms, which privilege or exclude sections of every ethno-cultural group.[11]

In conceptualising 'culture' among migrant youth for the case study reported in this book, we subscribed to Stivachtis' view that 'cultures are neither monolithic nor necessarily historically continuous', as the cultural values a migrant community claims to hold in common 'might be a contesting issue within that community', especially in the second generation.[12] While migrant communities culturally influence first- and second-generation youth in central or distant ways, it is misleading to assume a 'common culture', or the 'lumping of multiple identities into a monolithic entity such as race or ethnicity'.[13] One reason for this is that culture, when conflated with race and ethnicity, is 'conceptually and methodologically dubious' given that race and ethnicity are traditional demarcations of difference or 'otherness'.[14] Furthermore, 'different cultures always co-exist within cultures[15]', and so-called common cultures are typically further divided along generational, gendered, socio-economic and geographic lines to form 'overlapping cultures[16]' or sub-cultures.

Because 'multiple sources of cultural influence[17]' can and do exist within one person, the theoretical approach adopted for the research discussed in this book supports an individualistic conceptual approach to culture. In this, culture could be understood as 'a source of identity that situates individuals on the vast landscape of beliefs and perspectives that influence the way we interpret events, interact with others, and live our lives'.[18] Phrased differently, culture 'gives people a sense of who they are, of belonging, of how they should behave and what they should not be doing'.[19] This does not mean that culture should be viewed as static, autonomous or bounded as it 'develops through constant interconnection rather than in spite of it, and some form of multiculturalism, hybridity, and change is the normal state of human beings rather than a recent phenomenon'.[20] This 'activated, fluid and mobile nature of culture' is unconsciously absorbed through daily cultural encounters as well as consciously negotiated through 'agency', or will.[21] At the unconscious level, culture includes 'imprintings', or 'the imprints that culture makes on the minds of children … through its language, its norms, its assumptions, its beliefs, its values and its principles of intelligibility'.[22] Unconscious 'imprints' are also involuntarily acquired through exposure to mainstream and/or minority 'material culture' in the form of the media, sport and other leisure activities, food, the visual arts and architecture.[23] From an agency perspective, people are 'culture-and-meaning makers, constantly trying to understand and explain the environments we live in'.[24] For the children of immigrants, cultural meaning is negotiated by the extent to which they embrace their cultural heritage and by their selective absorption of the cultural values and beliefs of wider society, or aspects of it.[25] These processes of understanding and interpreting culture(s) are extremely diverse, not least because they invariably involve 'some level of reflection or confusion'.[26] This diversity of cultural experience and the key issues involved in conceptualising cultural diversity will be explored further in the context of Arab and Muslim youth in Australia.

While subject to the same range of experiences and the same exclusionary dialogue that faces adult Arab and Muslim Australians, young people also share specific sets of experiences and are subject to particular forms of exclusionary discourses. This was demonstrated in the previous chapter in discussion of the two incidents that occurred in Sydney within the last six years: the gang-rape case and the Cronulla riots. These incidents and their legacies demonstrate how Arab and Muslim Australian youth were identified, not necessarily correctly, with particular forms of stereotypical image-making, both by political elites and the mainstream media. Whether racialised and often mediated discourse about Arab and Muslim migrants can penetrate school boundaries is no longer in question. What is still being debated though is the correlation between school, external factors and students' overall educational experiences.

Schooling and Identity Formation

Identity formation is a central issue for migrant youth, regardless of how much time has elapsed since leaving their country of origin. This issue is particularly salient for first- and second-generation[27] migrant youth who negotiate identity space comfortably alongside, in opposition to, or, more commonly, somewhere in between their immigrant parents' conceptions of culture and the receiving mainstream culture in which they live. Unlike their non-migrant peers, first- and second-generation youth are exposed to intra-ethnic *and* inter-ethnic dynamics and experiences in their journey towards cultural-identity formation. These experiences are complex and diverse and are navigated within multilayered ethnic, racial, familial, gendered, socio-economic and educational contexts. In Australia, there has been growing scholarly interest in first- and second-generation migrant youth since the national move towards 'multiculturalism' in the late 1970s and early 1980s. This is not surprising given that one in five Australians is a second-generation migrant and most second-generation Australians from non-English-speaking backgrounds are currently in their twenties, teens, or younger.[28]

Cultural identity is perhaps best conceptualised as the 'juxtaposition of "self" and "other"' in terms of self-identity and its relation to wider society. From this initial singular concept, the individual is then situated within a wider 'group identity', from within which individuals subscribe '"to" and participate "in" agreed upon patterns of behaviour and ways of understanding'.[29] The evolution of this dynamic of cultural identification then functions across two broadly identified domains: the private and public. As cultural identity is such an integral part of oneself, 'it can be difficult to recognise our individual cultural perspective'.[30] Nonetheless, even limited cross-cultural contact can alter individual 'values, behaviours and attitudes[31]', which shape how migrant youth interpret and negotiate their present, past and future conditions and circumstances. How individuals see themselves lays the 'foundation for future perception, self-appraisal, and behaviour[32]' as identity conceptions shape imaginings about what constitutes 'the good life' or 'subjective well-being'.[33] Similarly, 'subjective perception and understanding of the communal past by each generation represent a defining element in the concept of cultural identity[34]' in the here and now.

Researchers who emphasise the importance of education in identity formation tend to adopt a holistic approach by positioning 'The School' within broader familial, gendered, cultural, ethnic, socio-economic and racial contexts. This is because there is general consensus that cultural identities are constructed both 'inside and outside the school arena' and that academic achievement is often contingent on youth interactions with the wider community.[35] These broader influences and structures shape the divergent ways that migrant youth perceive 'themselves and others who co-exist with them in schools[36]', as well as their attitudes towards education.[37] That is, cultural heritage influences school adjustment and patterns of engagement among migrant youth and vice versa. However, the school, as a 'public domain' of identity formation is like other public institutions in that it is subject to dominant cultural tropes. In the school setting these dominant cultural tropes are filtered through Government legislation and education policies; curriculum design assigned by the dominant culture; pedagogical practice derived from a dominant epistemological perspective; and, collectively, an overall educational template that affirms cultural compliance. Critical race theory (CRT) would argue that, as in legal institutional structures, 'whiteness' as a favoured notion is deeply imbedded, and 'blackness' or ethnic 'hybridity' sits at the margins. In the educational setting, being at the margins means a lowering of expectations around educational outcomes and possibly even participation. One way of dismantling the hegemony of 'whiteness' is through the construction of discursive counter-narratives. Through stories, young people are encouraged to build mutual understanding and recognition, a hypothesis that was tested in the research project that will be discussed further in Chapters 3 and 4.

Those who assert the primacy of education in migrant youth cultural identification tend to advance one of three key arguments. First, some argue that school, especially secondary school, strongly influences cultural identity because mid to late adolescence is commonly regarded as the most formative period in identity development.[38] It is during adolescence when a 'crisis of identity is most paramount in the mind of the young person[39]' and when the children of immigrants are especially likely to ask: 'Who am I?' Cultural identification also differs according to age as older adolescents typically have 'higher cultural identity levels' than younger migrant children.[40] As An Vo explains, first- and second-generation migrant youth 'do see cultural identity as an issue, especially in the years covered by secondary school'.[41] For second-generation youth, their capacity to develop a positive cultural identity during adolescence 'strongly influences school to workplace transitions' because cultural 'deficits and disadvantages confronted by second generation youth at age eighteen or twenty are far more difficult to overcome[42]' than those among their native peers.

Second, as others argue, school plays an important positive role in cultural-identity formation because of the large number of schools in multicultural societies that adopt integrative modes of acculturation.[43] This is to encourage migrant youth to acquire 'the skills needed for participation in the host culture along with adherence to traditional cultural patterns'.[44] Related to this viewpoint is the argument that migrant youth are 'better adjusted to school[45]' and value school more highly than students of the dominant culture. In part, this is seen as the outcome of integrative school cultures, in part because of 'the greater satiability within immigrant families', and in part because migrant parents often have 'higher aspirations' for their children.[46] For many migrant youth, 'the process of fulfilling their parents' dreams and creating a better future for themselves begins at school'.[47] Those who emphasise the positive impact of school on cultural identification often point to the higher aggregate educational attainment of immigrant children than native school children of comparable socio-economic status to justify their claim.[48] Assuming this, it follows that the educational trajectories of first- and second-generation migrant youth are more likely to result in positive forms of cultural identification based on greater opportunities for social integration through material success.[49] Higher education levels and better job opportunities could also 'buffer' migrant youth to varying degrees against the 'adversity experienced in migrating and settling in an often hostile homogenising and discriminating dominant host society'.[50]

Third, a number of academic studies have argued that the patterns of integration among first- and second-generation youth are extremely diverse and that positive representations fail to capture the complex processes of inclusion and exclusion in the school setting. Recent research has attempted to understand and explain these divergent paths to cultural identification in schools by focusing on the construct of a 'subjective identity[51]' or 'self-representation'.[52] This individualistic approach is premised on two assumptions: first, that the 'individual histories of all the students, consciousness of different identity, origin and cultural background … give value to each individual/member of the group', and second, that individual feelings of belonging to a group affect inter-group relationships.[53] In other words, the cultural frames of reference and identities of migrant youth are subjectively negotiated by the extent to which 'meaning is applied to self, others and the world'.[54]

Several studies suggest a positive correlation between self-identification and school performance. For example, Carola Suarez-Orozco found in her research on second-generation migrant youth that children who adopt a 'self-referential label that includes their parents' country of origin' tend to perform better at school and have 'different perceptions of discrimination and opportunities' than those who choose a 'pan ethnicity' (such as Hispanic or Asian), or who only identify themselves in terms of their host country (such as

Australian).[55] Gender also influences both identity construction and academic outcomes. For instance, Ruben Rumbaut's large-scale study of 5127 American youths (aged between twelve and seventeen) with Asian, Latin American and Caribbean backgrounds found that girls are more likely to choose a hyphenated cultural identity than boys.[56] Girls in most immigrant groups also tend to out-perform boys in their 'grades, academic engagement, high school completion and future aspirations'.[57] This gender-specific 'failure' by first- and second-generation males is often attributed to their inability to overcome 'conventional definitions of masculinity[58]', which may lead boys to regard school as 'a feminine institution where teachers favour girls in classroom settings'.[59] Other writings point to a 'crisis within middle-class masculinity that is fuelling the educational discourse of male disadvantage', causing boys to 'take refuge in a counter-culture of misbehaviour in schools[60]' or to focus on sport at the expense of homework. Another view is that boys are more concerned about 'differences in status and prestige which are related to groups in general and ethnic groups in particular'.[61] As a result, first- and second-generation migrant boys are statistically more likely to report and respond negatively to racism than girls, and to 'check out' of school after 'hostile' interactions with teachers and school administrators.[62]

Of course, it is misleading to simplistically conceptualise 'boys' or 'migrant boys' as single homogenous groups because 'masculinity', like 'femininity', is nuanced in a range of ways and subject to a range of influences, such as socio-economic, racial, ethnic and cultural. Many girls from traditional cultural backgrounds report that their greatest challenge is 'making their success acceptable within families and their own immigrant community'.[63] These 'cultural incongruities' between school and familial values and expectations can 'undermine successful learning'.[64] It is because of this diversity in gendered identities and educational outcomes that some argue against the 'popularist tendency to assert a binary oppositional and "competing victims" perspective' on the different school experiences, achievements and identities of boys and girls.[65]

The demography of student populations also affects how first- and second-generation youth publicly negotiates cultural identity. In Australia, migrant children who attend 'low-ethnic population primary and secondary schools' have been found to be less likely to address cultural identity issues than those who attend high-ethnic population schools, either due to pressure within the school to assimilate or to a lack of encouragement to retain their parents' cultural heritage.[66] Low-ethnic ratio schools are also less likely to offer the sorts of 'intercultural'[67] curricula and extra-curricular activities, such as classes that engage with their cultural heritage[68] or activities with community-based cultural organisations[69], which have been shown to promote healthy cultural identities in immigrant youth.

The lexical shift to 'intercultural education' from 'multicultural education', which began in the late 1970s, aimed to address pluralist concerns that multiculturalism did not properly combat racism and 'offered only a tokenistic understanding of non-dominant knowledge, denigrating cultural difference to the study of samosas, saris and steel bands'.[70] The term 'intercultural' was seen to express 'the ideal that cultures have a reciprocal influence on each other', as opposed to the more 'static' idea of multiculturalism.[71] Despite this, even highly culturally complex schools that claim to adopt an intercultural curriculum may only do so superficially in practice.

For example, Leeman and Ledoux found in their study of Dutch schools that although intercultural education has been compulsory in the Netherlands for more than two decades, very few schools have successfully adopted intercultural curricula. This was due to a lack of conceptual clarity on 'practical' suggestions for realisation, no strong public demand for school reform to introduce the intercultural in mainstream classrooms, and a teaching force that does not see the relevance of 'the intercultural'.[72] Gunther Dietz also observed in his study of Muslim minority students in Granada that the headmaster of a public primary school described his school's curriculum as 'intercultural' simply because it included other religions when celebrating festivals such as Christmas, which he claimed promoted 'mutual tolerance and inter-religious understanding'.[73] Tolerance and understanding, however, are not in themselves markers of cultural inclusion when culturally acceptable standards are set and controlled by the dominant ethnic group.[74]

The degree of ethnic and cultural heterogeneity in schools in turn affects the exposure by minority students to racism, and thus, their ability to develop positive cultural identities. Recent literature on non-European immigrant children has emphasised 'the problems of racism and the pressure to assimilate and subsequent root-culture loss[75]' as their key challenges in identity construction and projection in schools. High aspirations of migrant parents and desire by their children for a better life 'frequently prove insufficient in the face of assimilationist pressures, institutional racism, low teacher expectations and the many other barriers that minority youth too often encounter on the path to academic success'.[76] Prejudicial attitudes are unlikely to remain unchallenged when teachers, parents and other community leaders argue that 'There's no racism here', when what they actually mean is 'We have so few non-white children at school that we get few racist incidents'.[77] Minority children, too, often succumb to assimilationist pressures in predominantly white schools because they want acceptance from their peers.[78] In such situations, teachers may lack knowledge and/or interest in the cultural backgrounds of their minority students, make false 'assumptions about children's perceptions, knowledge and beliefs[79]', or themselves exhibit subtle or overt forms of racism. For instance, Hossein Adibi found in his study of young Iranian-Australians that they considered Iranian teachers to be 'more helpful and friendly' and that some 'were more worried about the racist attitudes of [Australian] teachers than of the students', especially following September 11.[80] Teacher–student relationships may also be either positively or negatively affected if ethnic-majority teachers discriminate against minority teachers, leading them to 'believe that they constantly need to "prove" their ability in the classroom and that they are treated in an overly-judgmental manner'.[81]

The impact of racism on youth cultural identification in the school environment varies considerably according to localised 'school cultures'. However, 'schools often operate as spaces where the realities of race and racism go undiscussed, even if understood by the students'.[82] Leaving racism unacknowledged can allow a drift to disengagement or low achievement for students feeling its effects. One method of confronting the issue of racism in schools is to call 'upon all parties, including students, to challenge shared assumptions'.[83] Using a strategy of engagement, the risk of 'being black in one classroom mean[ing] "low achieving" and in another "high achieving"' because of differing school policies, practices and modes of engagement with migrant communities and wider society cannot be left to chance.[84] While schools do not create racism and cannot prevent it, the type of school culture in place influences the extent to which teachers are prepared to combat discrimination in classrooms.[85] In part, these cultures are shaped by varying levels of teacher responsiveness to the 'complexity of children's social worlds and the dynamics of power and control that operate within it'.[86] They are also informed by the leadership and attitudes of school principals, systemic issues such as material resources and staffing, and by induction programs that 'socialise new teachers into the local norms and customs[87]', which in turn reflect the school's 'set of values and meanings'.

Schools as interactive sites of culture therefore need to bring all of its strands—people, structures and practices—into play in a way that is responsive not only to the school as a microcosm of society, but the wider social cultures. CRT theorists Solórzano and Villalpando identify five central points for recognition: (1) the centrality of racism, (2) the challenge to dominant ideology, (3) the commitment to social justice, (4) the importance of experiential knowledge, and (5) the use of an interdisciplinary perspective.[88]

Acknowledging the interactive power of these points in the classroom brings to the surface what is already there but is often disavowed. David Stovall employed these five principles in his design of a secondary-school program entitled 'Race, Class, Media and Chicago', in which the students were encouraged to speak freely about their experiences of racism in order to unpack the five points identified by Solórzano and Villalpando. Stovall found the media ideal for this purpose as it 'served as a space where race could be discussed and analysed' through a range of media forms 'from situation comedies to music videos', spaces that are often 'saturated with subtle racial innuendo and conjecture'.[89] However, Stovall's class also tackled the print media and reportage on issues such as street gangs in Chicago and coverage of the United States' Operation Iraqi Freedom, where students unearthed the media's use of stereotypes and the power these stereotypes have to obscure issues. One of the most important elements of his program Stovall found, however, was the opportunity it opened up for students to share perspectives and what he called their 'experiential knowledge'.[90]

Beyond school cultures, responses to racism in the school environment are negotiated individually and its impacts are felt to a variety of degrees. Exposure to racism plays varying roles in shaping the cultural identity of first- and second-generation migrant youth and their reactions to perceived discrimination takes many different forms. For example, one study found that while some Korean-American children responded to racial stereotypes of themselves as 'model minority' students by performing poorly academically, dropping out of school or joining gangs to dispel their 'freakish alter ego of geek and nerd', others embraced what they saw as their cultural values of 'education and hard work'.[91] Somewhat differently, many second-generation Filipina-Canadian girls responded to various forms of racism (such as being labelled 'Flips' and physically attacked) by committing suicide, while others coped with the inter-generational 'cascade of trauma' by weighing their own relatively 'easier' school experiences of discrimination against those of their migrant parents.[92]

Second-generation youth sometimes report pressure in the school environment to 're-identify with a wider cosmopolitan, transnational, often economically marginal and urban-based immigrant population'.[93] While 'cosmopolitan identities' may be positively negotiated in the sense that 'pan-ethnic identifications' could reduce intercultural barriers (and thus encourage new assertions of identity), they may equally reinforce negative racial stereotypes such as 'black'.[94] In its most positive form, 'cosmopolitanism' refers to a 'paradigm that values inclusion, tolerance and respect for the other', making it 'a plausible alternative to historical assimilationist/nativist practices'.[95] This interpretation has been promoted by a number of scholars including Stevenson[96], Walker and Serrano[97], and De Castro et al[98], who argue for a 'cosmopolitan approach to education' where there is a renewed emphasis on the values of diversity, tolerance, understanding and inclusion in educational institutions to encourage individual students 'to engage with their creative self[99]' in identity formation. While both multiculturalism and cosmopolitanism promote diversity and tolerance, 'cosmopolitans espouse the importance of multiple affiliations', whereas multiculturalists may not.[100] Indeed, as multiculturalism has fallen into disfavour, it has been replaced by the notion of citizenship which has now been incorporated into Australia's secondary-school curriculum. Citizenship and its strong identification with 'Australian values' (as we discussed in Chapter 1) might actually constrain the humanist, more universal, ideas of cosmopolitanism because of citizenship's close affiliation with nationalism. As Martha Nussbaum asks in her paper 'Patriotism and Cosmopolitanism':

> As students here grow up, is it sufficient for them to learn that they are above all citizens of the United States, but that they ought to respect the basic human rights of citizens of India, Bolivia, Nigeria, and Norway? Or should they, as I think—in addition to giving special attention to the history and current situation of their own nation—learn a good deal more than is frequently the case about the rest of the world in which they live …?[101]

An irreconcilable tension between cosmopolitanism and citizenship therefore seems to exist unless individuals are allowed—indeed encouraged—to embrace the many layers of community, ethnic, linguistic, religious and national identifications that become increasingly inevitable with increased migrant and refugee movement. Although the term 'cosmopolitanism' is not new, introduced as it was in 1928[102], it could be reasonably argued to constitute the 'new intercultural' in its modern educational context. Like intercultural educational strategies, genuinely cosmopolitan policies emphasise the need to 'follow an inclusive cultural strategy' that offers 'children a range of cultural repertoires', and 'seek to revalue cultural practices' that would be unacceptable in more traditional educational institutions.[103] In practice however, like 'multiculturalism', 'cosmopolitan' education policies may suffer from a lack of conceptual clarity, innovation and motivation, particularly at a time when anxieties over the 'other' are a consistent point of focus.

Understanding Arab and Muslim Australian Youth

When attempting to understand the impacts of social and political dynamics upon Arab and Muslim Australian youth identity formation, research in Australia has tended to emphasise sociological, rather than educational determinants. From the 1990s onwards a significant body of work emerged, coinciding with increased negative media attention directed towards Lebanese-Australian youth living in

Sydney.[104] A cultural studies approach towards such media reporting and political discourse has also influenced studies of Arab youth identity and representations in popular culture. This, combined with the sociological approach, has seen an ethnographic method of engaging with the identity constructions of Arab and Muslim Australian youth, which has focused on issues of social tension and marginalisation.

Of particular interest to these research approaches has been the integration/assimilation of young Lebanese-background men in south-west Sydney and the impact of local socio-political dynamics upon identity formation. Poynting, Noble, Tabar and Collins have attempted to deconstruct the stereotypes of young men from Lebanese backgrounds and examined how they intersect with the lived experiences and subjective identity formation of young men. They have found that young Lebanese-Australians are creative in their identity constructions, strategically positioning their various expressions of ethnic identity within a complex web of social relations. This type of research argues that when these social relations are experienced as racism or exclusion, young male Lebanese-Australians may exert forms of ethnic identity that are collective, resistant, and sometimes aggressively masculine and oppositional. These expressions of identity allow a marginalised ethnic minority group to experience a sense of power and collective solidarity in the face of racism and exclusion. This manifestation is a reflection of the call for solidarity when confronted by misunderstandings that a group feels powerless to correct, as advocated by Zachariah Matthews and Siddiq Buckley mentioned earlier.

A broader theoretical approach outside the socio-cultural paradigm has been missing from studies concerned with better understanding this group. But also Arab and Muslim Australian youth have received scant attention in educational research since the late 1970s, as a result of a burgeoning interest in multicultural education which absorbed them into a broader discourse on CALD (culturally and linguistically diverse) students' achievements. This has left a gap in better understanding the experiences of these particular groups in their critical formative years of secondary schooling. The vacant space left in the absence of that more nuanced understanding has been filled with narrow notions of Islam—such as problematised perceptions of gender and resistance to assimilation tropes—as the 'war on terror' since 2001 has overtaken any such dialogue. The conflation of cultural experience under the umbrella of CALD, coupled with a rise in suspicions surrounding the Muslim community, has therefore risked the further marginalisation of this group by way of a simple lack of awareness. For example, by the mid 1980s some Australian researchers were claiming that, in general, CALD students had achieved educational parity with their English-speaking-background (ESB) counterparts, yet professionals working with Lebanese-Australian students noted that they were suffering academically and not achieving similar levels of attainment as other groups.[105] The low educational achievements of Arab and Muslim Australian youth, particularly those of Lebanese background, have long been explained in educational research by limited English-language proficiency, schooling and social transitions for recently arrived students, and lack of adequate parental involvement in their education.[106]

More recently, a small number of studies have recognised that Arab and Muslim Australian students, on average, continue to achieve relatively low educational results, despite being long settled, second- or third-generation Australians.[107] While for many other CALD groups in Australia there has been a trend of upward educational mobility as settlement periods increase, this trend has bypassed students of Middle Eastern origin. Consequently, it has become less convincing for educational researchers and policy-makers to explain Arab and Muslim Australian students' low educational achievements in terms of linguistic difficulties and the challenges of adjusting to a new schooling environment. Most of these students enter the Australian schooling system at an early age, many having been born in Australia. It has been shown that by the age of ten, the overwhelming majority of Australian children are proficient in English, irrespective of their parents' English proficiency.[108] Educational research, then, is only just starting to explain and address the ongoing poor outcomes of Arab and Muslim Australian students. Researchers currently working in this area generally focus on measuring in-school factors affecting achievements, such as teacher–student relationships, cultural attitudes towards education, and family involvement in children's schooling. Much of this research attempts to find statistical correlations between the factors affecting students' attitudes towards education and their actual educational outcomes.[109]

The limited number of studies in Australia that have examined the educational experiences of Arab and Muslim Australian students have tended to focus on those who are newly arrived migrants to Australia, and much of this is limited to the Sydney context. Interest peaked following an influx of Lebanese migrants in the late 1970s and 1980s, prompting two commissioned reports published by the Australian Government Publishing Service. The focus of these studies was on newly arrived students of Lebanese and Turkish background. In 1980, a study on the education and employment outcomes of Turkish and Lebanese youth explored how these newly arrived groups adjusted to the Australian school system and workforce, and explored the factors that hindered or aided their adjustment.[110] Along the same lines, a study in 1983 looked into Lebanese students as a recently arrived, under-performing minority group.[111] This study reported a disjuncture between the high educational aspirations of Lebanese students and their families on the one hand, and their low academic outcomes and retention rates on the other. It found that 75 per cent of Lebanese students' parents encouraged university attendance, 42 per cent aspired to jobs in the upper professional category, and that those parents from CALD backgrounds attached greater importance to their child's schooling than ESB parents.[112] Running concurrently with these high aspirations, however, were poor academic outcomes and low rates of retention. For example, 27 per cent of Lebanese-origin students had high aspirations but failed to gain the Higher School Certificate—the equivalent of Victoria's VCE (Victorian Certificate of Education).[113]

The study accounted for this disjuncture between aspirations and outcomes in a number of ways. It suggested that CALD parents' high educational and career aspirations for their children often reflect the parents' view of the school as a 'socializing rather than an accrediting agency—the job of the school is to turn migrant children into Australians'.[114] In this sense, it challenged theories that argue that CALD parents' high aspirations for their children solely reflect a desire for the children to experience social and economic mobility in a way that the parents could not. Lebanese parents were consistent with other CALD parents who held high educational aspirations for their children, however, it also found that it was difficult for them to become involved in their child's education and to provide guidance on career choice. This reflected their English-language difficulties, a lack of information, remoteness from the school community, and an inability to source information about careers. Not only did language barriers prevent parents' involvement in the school community and their child's education, but many CALD parents found their family and job responsibilities too great to also balance with such involvement. These parents also reported that they lacked the necessary abilities, knowledge and skills to make a worthwhile contribution to their child's education and thought that education was 'best left to teachers'.[115]

In terms of a gendered view of the educational participation and achievement of Arab youth, an extensive study was undertaken in the late 1980s. The study cohort was made up of predominantly Lebanese and Egyptians[116], the fifth-largest ethnic group in Australia at that time, 85.4 per cent of whom continued to speak Arabic at home. This study found that Lebanese-background youth had relatively lower education rates than those of Egyptian background.[117] Girls were found to be outperformed by males, especially girls from Lebanese backgrounds who were more likely to withdraw from education in favour of marriage. Girls also expressed more negative schooling experiences than boys. Generally, Arab students reported problems at school in four major areas: language barriers to educational achievement and a lack of relevancy of subjects; lack of acceptance because of cultural, national or religious background; barriers due to non-English-speaking background; and an inability to make friends.[118]

In the 1990s, interest in the educational experiences and needs of Arab-Australian students waned, despite the continuation of their relatively low educational outcomes. The lack of research in this period reflects a move towards more generic multicultural educational research, rather than focusing on particular ethnic groups, together with a decrease in the number of Arabic-speaking migrants. One exception was a study published by Gibbons, White and Gibbons in 1994. It attempted to continue the Australian discourse around these students' educational needs with an investigation into the experience of Lebanese-Australian children at a disadvantaged Catholic primary school in Sydney.[119] At the beginning of the project, Year 3 teachers estimated that 40 to 50 per cent of Arabic-speaking-background students at the school were non-functional readers and writers. With the intervention of their project, this percentage was reduced to 10 to 15 per cent.[120] The student cohort were Lebanese from Catholic backgrounds, lived in an area of Sydney where the Lebanese community has tended to segregate, and were from low socio-economic backgrounds. This school, in association with the researchers, designed and implemented a series of educational strategies over a two-year period with the aim of ensuring that the Lebanese-background students achieved the same 'life choices and opportunities as other Australian children': 'If equality of outcome (rather than equality of opportunity only) is a goal of the school, and if all children, despite their linguistic background, have the right to achieve this equality, then the challenge is achieving linguistic and educational rights for all children'.[121]

The study reported difficulties in establishing project evaluation methods that could reflect the outcomes of curriculum changes and whether the project had long term impacts on life opportunities. It concluded that the education system needed to more adequately reflect the linguistic backgrounds and cultural rights of children in order for them to develop their full educational and social potential:

> To continue to resource these schools on the assumption that they are primarily monolingual and monocultural runs the risk of developing a second class citizenry which has never had the opportunity to develop to its fullest potential through the provision of appropriate educational programmes that acknowledge the linguistic rights of the children.[122]

This study represents one of the more recent investigations into the educational outcomes of Arabic-speaking-background students. To some extent, the demographic of the student cohort runs parallel with that of the study that we report on and discuss in the next chapter. Those likely to have lived in Australia for a number of years in socially segregated communities and socio-economically disadvantaged families tend to achieve limited education standards and qualifications, and consequently do not move beyond a low income range. However, there are important distinctions to be made between this study and that reported in Chapter 3. First, the study by Gibbons et al focuses on primary education rather than the 'at risk' secondary Years 9 and 10. As such, the strategies developed to engage students and their parents in a successful educational process are likely to be very divergent. Second, the Gibbons project was based on the assumption that linguistic barriers were central in influencing the poor educational outcomes of the Lebanese-Australian students.

More recent research published in 2002 into factors influencing the educational performance of students from socio-economically disadvantaged backgrounds suggests that the educational challenges for Arab and Muslim Australian students have not improved.[123] That is, the time period over which Arabic-speaking communities have established themselves in Australia has not impacted positively on the educational outcomes for children from these communities, despite the emphasis that earlier research gave to the language barriers they experienced. While other CALD groups have achieved educational mobility, this trend has not been perceived in relation to Arabic-speaking students.[124] For example, in 1996 Dobson, Birrell and Rapson argued that multicultural education policies focusing on delivering better educational outcomes for CALD students were misguided because CALD students had higher participation rates in secondary and tertiary education which, they argued, was achieved through educational mobility.[125] Yet their study revealed a great degree of variation in educational participation between ethnic groups. For example, while students from Vietnamese, Chinese, Eastern European and Korean backgrounds were more likely to be enrolled in higher education courses than ESB students, those from Arabic, Khmer and Turkish backgrounds were only half as likely to be participating in higher education as ESB students. Recent research has confirmed the continuation of this trend. Considine and Zappalà reported in 2002 that while CALD students were almost three times as likely as other students to gain outstanding results, students from Middle Eastern and African backgrounds were less likely than ESB and other CALD students to achieve outstanding results.[126]

In answering their main research question, which sought to determine the factors influencing the educational performance of students from socio-economically disadvantaged backgrounds, the Considine and Zappalà study concluded that within the low socio-economic status (SES) bracket, social rather than economic factors are more predictive of students' educational performance. In particular, it was argued that the level of parental education is a key predictor of student academic achievement.[127] This finding lends support to the notion advanced by some studies that, while both social and economic components of the SES equation may have distinct and separate influences on educational outcomes, social factors are more significant than economic factors in explaining children's educational outcomes and are among the most replicated results in child development studies.[128] Higher status families, some researchers suggest, foster a higher level of achievement and provide higher levels of psychological support for their children. The level of parental education was found to be strongly associated with factors such as the home literacy environment, parents' learning styles and investing in resources that promote learning such as quality child care, educational materials and visits to museums.[129] While families with low incomes face greater hurdles in achieving effective parenting, which in turn often harms their children's development and educational achievement[130], this study's approach supported the thesis that low income and linguistic factors are not the only barriers to children's strong educational results.[131]

Considine and Zappalà's research found that 'some ethnic groups seem to be more disadvantaged than others in terms of educational outcomes', for example students from Middle Eastern and African backgrounds[132], but did not proffer any suggestions as to why this may be. The important clue, however, may be in the consistent link among these groups between low socio-economic background and parents with little formal education. An investigation into second-generation Australians confirmed this, reporting that:

> … a significant proportion of children with parents from Lebanon, Turkey or Vietnam come from families of lower socioeconomic background, with fathers who are more likely to be employed in low skilled occupations or not

employed at all. Immigration from these three countries has largely been characterised by family or refugee migration rather than skilled migration.[133]

The issue of parent engagement at school and strategies for linking families more closely to their children's education is taken up in Chapter 4. The student focus of this study is explored in the next chapter, where we situate it within the wider influences of citizenship, identity and belonging in the prevailing environment of declining emphasis on multiculturalism, and discourses of fear stemming from the 'war on terror'.

Notes

1   E Baldwin et al. (eds), 1999, *Introducing Cultural Studies*, Prentice Hall Europe, UK, p. 137, cited in Tsai-Wei Chen, 2006, '"Sonic Constellations: Taiwanese Sojourners" Listening Experiences in London', *Organised Sound*, vol. 11, no. 1, p. 39.

2   WJ Lonner, 1984, 'Differing Views on 'Culture', *Journal of Cross-Cultural Psychology*, vol. 15, p.108, cited in Georgia T Chao and Henry Moon, 2005, 'The Cultural Mosaic: A Metatheory for Understanding the Complexity of Culture', *Journal of Applied Psychology*, vol. 90, no. 6, p. 1129.

3   Edward B Tylor in LH Morgan, 1877, *Ancient Society*, World Publishing, New York, cited in Bryan Page, 2005, 'The Concept of Culture: A Core Issue in Health Disparities', *Journal of Urban Health: Bulletin of the New York Academy of Medicine*, vol. 82, no. 2, Supplement 3, pp. iii–35.

4   Lisa Wedeen, 2002, 'Conceptualising Culture: Possibilities for Political Science', *American Political Science Review*, vol. 96, no. 4, p. 713.

5   Felicia Chigozie Anonyuo, 2006, Agency and Transnationalism: Social Organisation Among Young African Immigrants in the Atlanta Metropolitan Area, MA thesis, Georgia State University, Georgia, p. 12.

6   Josep Marti, 2005, 'The *Cultural Frames* Approach as an Alternative to the Ethnocratic Idea of Culture', Spanish Council for Scientific Research, www.anthroglobe.ca/docs/Cultural-Frames-as-Alternative-to-%20Ethnocratic-Idea-Culture.htm, last edited 23 September 2005, p. 3.

7   Abed Monawar, 2006, Cultural Assimilation Among Palestinian Immigrants in New Mexico, MA thesis, Texas Technical University, Texas, p. 7.

8   Kamaldeep Bhui, Stephen Stansfeld, Jenny Head, Mary Haines, Sheila Hillier, Stephanie Taylor, Russell Viner and Robert Booy, 2005, 'Cultural Identity, Acculturation and Mental Health among Adolescents in East London's Multiethnic Community', *Journal of Epidemiology and Community Health*, vol. 59, p. 297.

9   Val Colic-Peisker and Farida Tilbury, 2007, *Refugees and Employment: The Effect of Visible Difference on Discrimination*, Final Report, Centre for Social and Community Research, Murdoch University, Perth, p. 32.

10   Susan Wright, 1998, 'The Politicisation of Culture', *Anthropology Today*, vol. 14, p. 10, cited in Monawar, p. 8.

11   Sia Spiliopoulou Akermark, 2007, 'Multiculturalism in Crisis?', 'III Human Rights Congress, Human Rights in Diversity', Deusto, pp. 2, 5.

12   Yannis A Stivachtis, 2006, 'The International Order in a Multicultural World: Challenges for the "International" University', paper presented at '3rd Mid Atlantic Conference on the Scholarship of Diversity', Blacksburg, Virginia, 2–3 February, p. 2.

13   LI Bartlome and DP Macedo, 1997, 'Dancing with Bigotry: The Poisoning of Racial and Ethnic Identities', Harvard Educational Review, vol. 67, no. 2, p. 224, cited in Research Utilisation Support and Help (RUSH), 1999, *Disability, Diversity, and Dissemination. A Review of the Literature on Topics Related to Increasing the Utilisation of Rehabilitation Research Outcomes among Diverse Consumer Groups*, April, p. 4, www.researchutilization.org/matrix/resources/ddd/DisabilityDiversity.pdf.

14   Yoosun Park, 2005, 'Culture as Deficit: A Critical Analysis of the Concept of Culture in Contemporary Social Work Discourse', *Journal of Sociology and Social Welfare*, September, p. 7.

15   Antonella Surbone, 2004, 'Cultural Competence: Why?' *Annals of Oncology*, vol. 15, p. 697.

16   Melita Richter Malabotta, 2005, 'Managing Cultural Transitions: Multiculturalism, Interculturalism and Minority Policies', in Nada Svob-Dokic (ed.), *The Emerging Creative Industries in Southern Europe*, Institute for International Relations, Zagreb, p. 114.

17   Chao and Moon, p. 1129.

18   Saha Somnath, 2006, 'The Relevance of Cultural Distance Between Patients and Physicians to Racial Disparities in Health Care', *Journal of General Internal Medicine*, vol. 21, no. 2, p. 204.

19   P Harris and RT Moran, 1991, *Managing Cultural Differences*, 3rd edn, Gulf Publishing, Houston, p. 12, cited in Victor J Friedman and Ariane Berthoin Antal, 2005, 'Negotiating Reality: A Theory of Action Approach to Intercultural Competence', *Management Learning*, vol. 36, no. 1, p. 71.

20   Ben Feinberg, 2006, 'The Promise and Peril of Public Anthropology', *Human Rights & Human Welfare*, vol. 6, p. 168.

21   Adam Arvidsson, 2005, 'What is Culture?', in Karen M Ekstrom and Helene Brembeck (eds), *Elusive Consumption in Retrospect. Report from the Conference*, CFK-Rapport, p. 80, www.hgu.gu.se/files/cfk/rappporter/elusive%20consumption%20in%20retrospect.pdf.

22   Edgar Morin, 2006, 'Speech', in *What UNESCO for the Future? Forum of Reflexion*, Social and Human Sciences Sector, The United Nations Educational, Scientific and Cultural Organisation, Paris, p. 30.

23   See, for example, Jennifer Wenshya Lee and Yvonne M Hebert, 2006, 'The Meaning of Being Canadian: A Comparison Between Youth of Immigrant

and Non-Immigrant Origins', *Canadian Journal of Education*, vol. 29, no. 2, pp. 497–520, 501; Basildon Council, 2006, *'Culture Counts.' A Cultural Strategy for Basildon District*, Essex, United Kingdom, p. 9, www. basildon.gov.uk/80256B7500420D16/vWeb/flEFEN6U2KQE/$file/basild on+district+council+-+cultural+strategy+2006+-+full+version.pdf; and Gordon Waitt, Rebecca M Galea and Patrick Rawstone, 2001, 'Generation and Place of Residence in the Symbolic and Lived Identity of Maltese in Sydney, Australia', *Australian Geographer*, vol. 32, no. 1, pp. 78.

24   Daniel Duffy, 2006, 'Autonomy, Representation and *Lekil Kuxlejal* in Highland Chiapas', in *Alone With Five Others: Dispatches from a Changing World*, The International Centre for Ethics, Justice and Public Life, Brandeis University, p. 20.

25   John W Berry, 2006, *Breakfast on the Hill. Petit Dejeuner sur la Colline. Fitting In: A Place for Immigrant Teens in Canadian Society*, Canadian Federation for the Humanities and Social Sciences, Ottawa, Ontario, p. 3.

26   Melissa Butcher, 2004, 'Universal Processes of Cultural Change: Reflections on the Identity Strategies of Indian and Australian Youth', *Journal of Intercultural Studies*, vol. 25, no. 3, p. 216.

27   While acknowledging that some scholars have been critical of the term 'second generation', this study does not intend to infer that the second generation are 'people under investigation' or perpetual foreigners, as John Hutnyk, among others, suggest. John Hutnyk, 'The Dialectic of Here and There: Anthropology "at Home" and British Asian Communism', *Social Identities*, vol. 11, no. 4, p. 351.

28   In 1996, there were 3.4 million second-generation Australians out of a total population of 17.6 million. Almost half of this number were of British origin, followed by second-generation Australians of Italian, New Zealand, Greek and Dutch origins. Siew-Ean Khoo, Peter McDonald, Dimi Giorgas and Bob Birrell, *Second Generation Australians*, Report for the Department of Immigration and Multicultural Affairs (DIMIA), www.dimia.gov.au/media/publications/multicultural/2gen/sg_ australians.pdf, April 2002, p. 9.

29   Kimasi L Browne, 'Identity, Scene, and Material Culture: The Place of African American Rare Soul Music on the British Northern Soul Scene', paper presented at the conference 'Manchester: Music and Place', Manchester, England, Manchester Institute for Popular Culture, Manchester Metropolitan University, www.soul-source.co.uk/ soul-words/soul-or-nothing-paper-given-manchester-universty.htm, 8 June 2006.

30   Joy L Lei, 2006, 'Teaching and Learning with Asian American and Pacific Islander Students', *Race, Ethnicity and Education*, vol. 9, no. 1, p. 91.

31   Jasmin Tahmaseb McConatha and Paul Stoller, 2006, 'Moving out of the Market: Retirement and West African Immigrant Men in the United States', *Journal of Intercultural Studies*, vol. 27, no. 3, p. 260.

32   Dena Phillips Swanson, Margaret Beale Spencer, Vinay Harpalani, Davido Dupree, Elizabeth Noll, Sofia Ginzburg and Gregory Seaton, 2003, 'Psychosocial Development in Racially and Ethnically Diverse

Youth: Conceptual and Methodological Challenges in the 21st Century', *Development and Psychopathology*, vol. 15, p. 749.

33   Ed Diener, Shigehiro Oishi and Richard E Lucas, 2003, 'Personality, Culture and Subjective Well-Being: Emotional and Cognitive Evaluations of Life', *Annual Review of Psychology*, vol. 54, pp. 403–25.

34   Anthony D Smith, 'National Identity and the Idea of European Unity', *International Affairs*, vol. 68, no. 1, p. 58, cited in Rawi Abdelal, Yoshiko M Herrera, Alastair Iain Johnston and Rose McDermott, *Identity as a Variable*, www.ucd.ie/euiteniba/pdf/Identity%20as%20a%20Variable.pdf, 22 July 2005, p.8.

35   Diego Herrera, 2003, 'School Success of Moroccan Youth in Barcelona: Theoretical Insights for Practical Questions', *Anthenea Digital*, vol. 4, p. 97.

36   Josephine Cafagna, Teresa Crea, Anna Maria Dell'oso, Melina Marchetta, Maria Pallotta-Chiarolli and Virginia Trioli, 2000, *Panel Discussion on Exploring Identity and Community Through the Arts and Culture*, 25 May, p. 806, www.iai.com.au/Exploring%20Identity.pdf.

37   Karmela Liebkind, Inga Jasinskaja-Lahti and Erling Solheim, 2004, 'Cultural Identity, Perceived Discrimination, and Parental Support as Determinants of Immigrants' School Adjustments: Vietnamese Youth in Finland', *Journal of Adolescent Research*, vol. 19, no. 6, p. 637.

38   Elizabeth Vaquera and Grace Kao, 2006, 'The Implications of Choosing "No Race" on the Salience of Hispanic Identity: How Racial and Ethnic Backgrounds Intersect Among Hispanic Adolescents', *The Sociological Quarterly*, vol. 47, p. 379.

39   Amado M Padilla, 2006, 'Bicultural Social Development', *Hispanic Journal of Behavioural Sciences*, vol. 28, no. 4, p. 471.

40   Nazilla Khanlou, 2005, 'Cultural Identity as Part of Youth's Self-Concept in Multicultural Settings', *International Journal of Mental Health and Addiction*, vol. 3, no. 2, p. 3.

41   An Vo, 2003, *Don't Throw Another Shrimp on the Barbie or Cultural Identity Matters!*, www.thesource.gov.au/involve/NYR/word/reports_social/a_vo.doc, p. 3.

42   Mark J Miller, 2006, *Opportunities and Challenges for Migrant and Migrant-Background Youth in Developed Countries*, short version report submitted to the United Nations Social and Economic Council, 15 July, p. 17.

43   Vije Franchi and Anne Andronikof-Sanglade, 2001, 'Intercultural Identity Structure of Second Generation French Women of African Descent', in Simon Bekker, Martine Dodds and Meshack M Khosa (eds), *Shifting African Identities*, Identity? Theory, Politics, History, Human Sciences Research Council, Pretoria, p. 117.

44   Jasinskaja-Lahti Liebkind and Solheim, p. 635.

45   ibid.

46   Hossein Adibi, 2003, 'Identity and Cultural Change: The Case of Iranian Youth in Australia', paper presented at the conference 'Social Change in the 21st Century', Centre for Social Change Research, Queensland University of Technology, 21 November, p. 8.

47   Krista M Perreira, Kathleen Mullan Harris and Doohan Lee, 2006, 'Making It in America: High School Completion by Immigrant and Native Youth', *Demography*, vol. 43, no. 3, p. x.

48   Ursula Keller, 2006, *Post-Secondary Educational Attainment of Immigrant and Native Youth*, Centre for Demography and Population Health, University of Florida, p. 2.

49   S Worbs, 2003, 'The Second Generation in Germany: Between School and Labor Market', *International Migration Review*, vol. 37, no. 4, pp. 1011–38; P Fernández-Kelly and L Konczal, 2005, 'Murdering the Alphabet: Identity and Entrepreneurship among Second Generation Cubans, West Indians, and Central Americans', *Ethnic and Racial Studies*, vol. 28, no. 6, pp.1153–81, 1157; L Pries, 2003, 'Labour Migration, Social Incorporation and Transmigration in the Old and New Europe: The Case Germany in a Comparative Perspective', *Transfer*, vol. 9, no. 3, pp.432–51, 12.

50   Franchi and Andronikof-Sanglade, p. 117.

51   Annick Prieur, 2002, 'Gender Remix: On Gender Constructions among Children of Immigrants in Norway', *Ethnicities*, vol. 2, no. 1, p. 53.

52   International Youth Summit 2001, *United to Combat Racism: A Youth Vision!*. Final Declaration and Plan of Action, Durban South Africa, 26 August – 8 September, p. 22.

53   Anna Aluffi Pentini, Beatrice Roselletti, Maria Ando, Lucia Tardani, Emilliano Bozzelli, Brigita Zepa, Inese Supule, Nuria Balliu Castanyer, Bru Pellissa, Nils Pagels and Holk Stobbe, *Youth and Inter Ethnic Schools. Actions Against Inter Ethnic Violence among Pupils at School. A Practical Handbook*, p. 42, www.bszi.lv/downloads/resources/DAPHNE/ Good%20practices_English.pdf, viewed 18 June 2007.

54   Jennifer Elsden-Clifton, 2006, 'Constructing "Thirdspaces": Migrant Students and the Visual Arts', *Studies in Learning, Evaluation, Innovation and Development*, vol. 3, no. 1, p. 1.

55   Carola Suarez-Orozco, 2003, 'Formulating Identity in a Globalised World', in Marcelo M Suarez- Orozco and Desiree Qin-Hilliard (eds), *Globalisation: Culture and Education in the New Millennium*, University of California Press and Ross Institute, California, p. 6.

56   Ruben G Rumbaut, 1994, 'The Crucible Within: Ethnic Identity, Self-Esteem and Segmented Assimilation among Children of Immigrants', *International Migration Review*, vol. 28, pp. 784–94.

57   Desiree Baolian Qin, 2006, 'The Role of Gender in Immigrant Children's Educational Adaptation', *Current Issues in Comparative Education*, vol. 9, no. 1, p. 9.

58   RW Connell, 2003, *The Role of Men and Boys in Achieving Gender Equality*, United Nations Division for the Advancement of Women (DAW) in collaboration with International Labour Organisation (ILO), the Joint United Nations Programmes on HIV/AIDS (UNAIDS) and the United Nations Development Programme (UNPD), Brasilia, Brazil, 7 October: pp. 5, 8.

59   Qin, p. 10.

60   G Weiner, M Arnot and M David, 1997, 'Is the Future Female? Female
     Success, Male Disadvantage and Changing Gender Patterns in
     Education', in AH Halsey, P Brown and H. Lauder (eds), *Education,
     Economy, Culture and Society*, Oxford University Press, Oxford, p. 627,
     cited in Victoria Foster, 1998, 'Gender, Schooling Achievement and
     Post-School Pathways: Beyond Statistics and Populist Discourse', paper
     presented at the conference 'Australian Association for Research and
     Education', Adelaide, South Australia, December.

61   B Kinke and M Verkuyten, 1997, 'Levels of Ethnic Self-Identification and
     Social Context', *Social Psychology Quarterly*, vol. 60, p. 351, cited in
     Khanlou, p. 11.

62   Carola Suarez-Orozco and Desiree Baolian Qin-Hilliard, 2003,
     'Immigrant Boys' Experiences in US Schools', in Niobe Way and
     Judy Y Chu (eds), *Adolescent Boys in Context*, New York University Press,
     New York, p. 10.

63   Michael S Merry, 2005, 'Social Exclusion of Muslim Youth in Flemish and
     French-Speaking Schools', *Comparative Education Review*, vol. 49, no. 1,
     p. 11.

64   Rebecca Novick, 1999, *Family Involvement & Beyond. School-Based Child
     and Family Support Programs*, Northwest Regional Educational
     Laboratory, Portland, p. 33.

65   Wayne Martino and Bob Meyenn, 2001, 'Preface', in Wayne Martino and
     Bob Meyenn (eds), *What about the Boys? Issues of Masculinity in Schools*,
     Open University Press, Buckingham and Philadelphia, p. xii.

66   Vo, p. 3.

67   Lee Dunn and Michelle Wallace, 2006, 'Australian Academics and
     Transnational Teaching: An Exploratory Study of Their Preparedness and
     Experiences', *Higher Education and Research Development*, vol. 25, no. 4,
     p. 360.

68   P Vedder, G Horenczyk and K Liebkind, 2006, *Ethno-Culturally Diverse
     Education Settings: Problems, Challenges and Solutions*, European
     Association for Research on Learning and Instruction, p. 6, www.earli.
     org/resources/Position%20Paper%202%20Ethno-culturally%20diverse%
     20education%20settings.pdf.

69   Joanna Ochocka et al., 2006, *Pathways to Success. Immigrant Youth at
     High School*, Centre for Research and Education in Human Services,
     Wilfrid Laurier University, Ontario, pp. 22–3.

70   David Coulby, 2006, 'Intercultural Education: Theory and Practice',
     Intercultural Education, vol. 17, no. 3, p. 245.

71   YAM Leeman, 2003, 'School Leadership for Intercultural Education',
     Intercultural Education, vol. 14, no. 1, p. 32.

72   Yvonne Leeman and Guuske Ledoux, 2003, 'Intercultural Education in
     Dutch Schools', *Curriculum Inquiry*, vol. 33, no. 4, p. 388.

73   Gunther Dietz, 2004, 'Frontier Hybridisation or Culture Clash?
     Transnational Migrant Communities and Sub-National Identity Politics
     in Andalusia, Spain', *Journal of Ethnic and Migration Studies*, vol. 30,
     no. 6, p. 1101.

74   Leeman and Ledoux, p. 388.

75   Peter Wakholi, 2005, African Cultural Education: A Dialogue with African
     Migrant Youth in Western Australia. MEd thesis, Murdoch University,
     Perth, p. 3.

76   Margaret A Gibson, 2005, 'Promoting Academic Engagement among
     Minority Youth: Implications from John Ogbu's Shaker Heights
     Ethnography', *International Journal of Qualitative Studies in Education*,
     vol. 18, no. 5, p. 583.

77   Elanor Knowles and Wendy Ridley, 2006, *Another Spanner in the Works:
     Challenging Prejudice and Racism in Mainly White Schools*, Trentham
     Books Limited, Oakhill, England, Stirling, USA, p. 1.

78   Anne Greer and Wenh In Ng, 2004, 'Beyond Bible Stories: The Role of
     Culture Specific Myths/Stories in the Identity Formation of Nondominant
     Immigrant Children', *Religious Education*, vol. 99, no. 2, p. 128.

79   Jim Harvey, 1996, 'Distance, Isolation and Place: A Study of Youth Living
     in a Remote Mining Community', paper presented at the 'Educational
     Research: Building New Partnerships' (ERA: AARE) Conference,
     Singapore, 25–29 November.

80   Adibi, p. 8.

81   Tehmina M Basit and Olwen McNamara, 2004, 'Equal Opportunities of
     Affirmative Action? The Induction of Ethnic Minority Teachers', *Journal
     of Education for Teaching*, vol. 30, no. 2, p. 98.

82   David Stovall, 2007, 'Where the Rubber Hits the Road: CRT goes to High
     School', in Adrienne D Dixson and Celia K Rousseau (eds), *Critical Race
     Theory in Education: All God's Children Got a Song*, Routledge,
     Abingdon, p. 233.

83   ibid.

84   Mariette de Haan and Ed Elbers, 2004, 'Minority Status and Culture:
     Local Constructions of Diversity in a Classroom in the Netherlands',
     Intercultural Education, vol. 15, no. 4, p. 442.

85   Sigrid Luchtenberg, 1998, 'Identity Education in Multicultural Germany',
     Journal of Multilingual and Multicultural Development, vol. 19, no. 1,
     p. 60.

86   Dympna Devine and Mary Kelly, 2006, '"I Just Don't Want to Get Picked
     on by Anybody": Dynamics of Inclusion and Exclusion in a Newly Multi-
     Ethnic Irish Primary School', *Children & Society*, vol. 20, no. 2, p. 128.

87   Basit and McNamara, p. 112.

88   ibid., p. 234.

89   Stovall, p. 235.

90   ibid., p. 238.

91   Hui Soo Chae, 2003, 'Talking Back to the Asian Model Minority
     Discourse: Korean-Origin Youth Experiences in High School', *Journal of
     Intercultural Studies*, vol. 25, no. 1, pp. 60, 67.

92   Geraldine Pratt, 2002, *Between Homes: Displacement and Belonging for
     Second Generation Filipina-Canadian Youths*, Research on Immigration
     and Integration in the Metropolis Working Paper Series no. 2–13,
     Vancouver Centre of Excellence: pp. 4–5, 17.

93   Timothy Sieber, 2005, 'Popular Music and Cultural Identity in the Cape
      Verdean Post-Colonial Diaspora', *Ethnographica*, vol. IX, no. 1, p. 145.
94   ibid., pp. 133, 145.
95   Jeffrey P Walker and Ana M Serrano, 2006, 'Formulating a Cosmopolitan
      Approach to Immigration and Social Policy: Lessons from American
      (North and South) Indigenous and Immigrant Groups', *Current Issues in
      Comparative Education*, vol. 9, no. 1, p. 60.
96   Nick Stevenson, 2003, 'Cultural Citizenship in the 'Cultural' Society:
      A Cosmopolitan Approach', *Citizenship Studies*, vol. 7, no. 3, p. 342.
97   Walker and Serrano, pp. 60–8.
98   Rui Vieira de Castro, Paula Guimarces and Amelia Vitoria Sancho, 2006,
      'Contributions to the Outline of a Training Device for Adult Educators',
      in Tiina Jaager and John Irons (eds), *Towards Becoming a Good Adult
      Educator – A Recourse Book for Adult Educators*, AGADE, Budapest, p. 19.
99   Richard Lee, 2005, *Youth, Citizenship and Modern Society: A Study of the
      Engaging Young People Project in East Cleveland*, Working Paper no. 75,
      Centre for Rural Economy, University of Newcastle Upon Tyne, UK, p. 20.
100   DA Hollinger, 1995, *Postethnic America: Beyond Multiculturalism*, Basic
      Books, New York, pp. 3–4, 84–6, cited in Walker and Serrano, p. 62.
101   Martha C Nussbaum, 'Patriotism and Cosmopolitanism' in Joshua
      Cohen (ed), *For Love of Country: Debating the Limits of Patriotism*,
      Beacon Press, Boston, 1996, p. 6.
102   Ameena Ghaffar-Kucher, 2006, 'Assimilation, Integration and Isolation?
      (Re) Framing the Education of Immigrants', *Current Issues in
      Comparative Education*, Teachers College, University of Columbia,
      www.tc.columbia.edu/cice/Current/9.1/91_edintro.html.
103   Stevenson, p. 342.
104   Compare to Jock Collins, Greg Noble, Scott Poynting and Paul Tabar,
      2000, *Kebabs, Kids, Cops and Crime: Ethnicity, Youth and Crime*, Pluto
      Press Australia, Annandale; also Greg Noble, Scott Poynting and Paul
      Tabar, 1999, 'Youth, Ethnicity and the Mapping of Identities: Strategic
      Essentialism and Strategic Hybridity among Male Arabic-Speaking Youth
      in South-Western Sydney', *Communal/Plural*, vol. 7, no. 1, pp. 29–44; and
      Scott Poynting, Greg Noble and Paul Tabar, 1999, '"Intersections" of
      Masculinity and Ethnicity: A Study of Male Lebanese Immigrant Youth in
      Western Sydney', *Race Ethnicity and Education*, vol. 2, no. 1, pp. 59–77.
105   D Cahill, 1996, *Immigration and Schooling in the 1990s.* Canberra,
      Australian Government Publishing Service, p. 35–42.
106   Compare to C Young, M Petty and A Faulkner, 1980, *Education and
      Employment of Turkish and Lebanese Youth*, Australian Government
      Publishing Service, Canberra; also P Meade, 1983, *The Educational
      Experiences of Sydney High Schools Students Report no. 3: A Comparative
      Study of Migrant Students of Non-English-Speaking Origin and Students
      Whose Parents Were Born in an English-Speaking Country, vol. 3*,
      Australian Government Publishing Service, Canberra; IA Duhou and
      R Teese, 1992, *Education, Work Force and Community Participation of
      Arab Australians: Egyptians, Lebanese, Palestinians and Syrians*,

Australian Government Publishing Service, Canberra; B Horvath, 1987,
'VARBRUL Analysis in Applied Linguistics: A Case Study', *Australian
Review of Applied Linguistics*, vol. 10, no. 2, pp. 59–67; and J Gibbons,
W White and P Gibbons, 1994, 'Combating Educational Disadvantage
among Lebanese Australians', in T Skutnabb-Kangas and R Phillipson
in collaboration with M Rannut (eds), *Linguistic Human Rights:
Overcoming Linguistic Disadvantage*, Mouton de Gruye, Berlin.
107 G Considine and G Zappalà, 2002, 'Factors Influencing the Educational
Performance of Students from Disadvantaged Backgrounds', in T Eardley
and B Bradley (eds), *Competing Visions: Refereed Proceedings of the
National Social Policy Conference 2001*, SPRC Report 1/02, University of
New South Wales, Sydney; see also S-E Khoo, P McDonald, D Giorgas
and B Birrell, 2002, *Second Generation Australians: Report for the
Department of Immigration and Multicultural and Indigenous Affairs*,
Department of Immigration and Multicultural and Indigenous Affairs,
Canberra, April, www.immi.gov.au/media/publications/multicultural/
2gen/index.htm, viewed 18 June 2007; and R Suliman and
DM McInerney, 2003, 'Motivational Goals and School Achievement:
Lebanese-Background Students in South-Western Sydney', paper
presented at the conference 'Australian Association for Research in
Education/New Zealand Association for Research in Education Joint
Conference 2003', Auckland, New Zealand.
108 Khoo et al; ibid.
109 Suliman and McInerney.
110 Young, Petty and Faulkner.
111 Meade.
112 ibid., p. 102.
113 ibid., p. 158.
114 ibid., p. 58.
115 ibid., p. 184.
116 Duhou and Teese, p. xvii.
117 ibid., p. xxi.
118 ibid., p. xxvi.
119 Gibbons, White and Gibbons; ibid.
120 ibid., p. 264.
121 ibid., p. 255.
122 ibid., p. 262.
123 Considine and Zappalà.
124 ibid., p. 95.
125 I Dobson, B Birrell and V Rapson, 1996, 'The Participation of Non-
English-Speaking-Background Person in Higher Education', *People and
Place*, vol. 4, no. 1, pp. 46–54.
126 Considine & Zappalà, p. 99.
127 ibid., p. 104.
128 JP Shonkoff and DA Phillips (eds), 2000, *From Neurons to Neighborhoods*,
National Academy Press, Washington, DC.

129   Shonkoff and Phillips.
130   Laura E. Berk, 1997, *Child Development*, Allyn & Bacon, Boston, p. 549.
131   Considine & Zappalà, p. 104.
132   ibid., p. 105.
133   Khoo et al, p. 5.

Educational Experiences of Arab and Muslim Australians

An Empirical Approach

In the previous chapter we discussed the key theoretical frameworks for conceptualising cultural identity, schooling and educational achievements and surveyed earlier research into Arab and Muslim youth in Australia. In this chapter we examine how migrant youth negotiate cultural identity in school environments and in the wider public realm to situate their experience within the prevailing social climate in order to understand its influence on educational and behavioural outcomes.

The argument presented in this chapter is fourfold. First, that the concepts of race and cultural identity can only be properly understood in individualistic terms, as opposed to the artificial construct of a 'common culture'. Second, that migrant youth responses to their cultural heritage and the societal mainstream are fluid and dynamic and are continually formed and re-evaluated at different points in their life cycles. Third, that while the global trend towards adopting multicultural, intercultural and cosmopolitan policies has been partly aimed at encouraging positive cultural-identity development in migrant youth, in practice such policies often fail to defend the inclusive values of tolerance, understanding and diversity they claim to embrace. Fourth, that the cultural messages conveyed by mainstream and minority/ethnic media can either assist or impede the processes of cultural-identity formation among migrant youth. Even limited negative messages from media agencies may be interpreted in divergent ways ranging from angry rejection to enthusiastic consumption if migrant youth feel disconnected from their cultural heritage or desire mainstream acceptance.

Race, Cultural Identity and Educational Achievement

Some of the most recent work on the factors affecting the educational achievement of students of Arabic-speaking background has been undertaken in south-west Sydney.[1] This community in Australia has grown considerably in recent years and is represented significantly in Melbourne's outer north-western suburbs. In the current, post-2001, political climate we expand our focus from Arab-Australians to Arab and Muslim Australian youth. It is difficult to define any cultural or religious group within the narrow confines of single concepts of identity, especially in a globalised age of human dislocation which can compel individuals to embrace a multiplicity of affiliations. As definitive terms therefore, 'Arab', 'Muslim' and 'Arab-Muslim' Australians are fraught with ambiguity. They infer homogeneity across Australia's Arabic-speaking and Muslim communities, which simply does not exist, and which contradicts the complexities of ethnicity, national origin and religious affiliations within these communities. For example, a person born in Iraq of Assyrian ethnicity and Christian faith will also most likely speak Arabic, but will not fit assumptions of being, as an Iraqi, either 'Arab' or 'Muslim'. Similarly, Muslims of South or Southeast Asian background would not fit such a grouping, although they can be similarly characterised in Australia, and so their experiences are often comparable. However, unlike the earlier studies discussed which specifically focused on 'Arab-Australians', the study reported in this book (hereafter the *Diversity Project*) expands its context to include Muslims as more relevant, not only to the student cohort in the schools, but to the prevailing social discourses as outlined in Chapter 1. We, therefore, acknowledge as implicit the heterogeneity of the Arab and Muslim Australian communities, but must nevertheless resort to a mode of 'naming' that incorporates both Arabs and Muslims. The term AMA—denoting Arab and Muslim Australians—is therefore used in our discussion of the *Diversity*

Project (in particular in data tables) it is the most accurate and concise definition for the community engaged in the research. It is also important to qualify at the outset, though, that the Muslims participating in the project, while of different nationalities, were all of Arabic-speaking background.

The *Diversity Project* attempted a more holistic approach to managing cultural diversity in education. It differed from other Australian research outlined in the previous chapter, which tended to focus mainly on individual students rather than their wider school, cultural, social, economic, political and familial contexts. The statistical approach to educational achievement may reflect the motivation levels of student cohorts; however, inappropriate or unrealised motivational goals may be only one factor hindering educational performance. In the context of the work on Lebanese-background students in Sydney, it has been argued that while CALD students in Australia tend to achieve good educational results in broad terms, Arabic-speaking background students are one subset of this group who consistently under-perform. Overall, recent research undertaken across Australia aimed to counter prevailing school-teacher views that the students are not motivated, have discipline problems and their parents are not supportive of their children's education and the school system. It was these factors that the *Diversity Project* sought to investigate, taking a more comprehensive view that encompassed the impacts of familial environment, cultural background, and teaching approaches.

The *Diversity Project* is also differentiated from the studies discussed in Chapter 2 in other ways. First, very importantly, it examined the educational needs and experiences of Arab and Muslim students both born in Australia and those who have recently arrived. The educational issues facing these groups today are likely to be different from the challenges facing newly arrived young people from Lebanon in the 1970s and 1980s. However, the same key problem of high educational aspirations and low academic outcomes remains. This suggests that these earlier challenges of educating recently arrived migrant children have been eclipsed by other more endemic, complex factors. For example, the *Diversity Project* is unable to sustain similar linguistic assumptions as were found in the Gibbons research outlined in the previous chapter.

The second differentiating factor of the *Diversity Project* was its focus on students in Years 9 and 10, the period identified as 'at risk' in the secondary-school years. The term 'at risk' has several connotations, but for this study it specifically meant at risk in educational terms: of dropping out of school; of not completing studies; and/or disengaging from school. The evidence suggests that low literacy and numeracy levels form only one factor affecting the educational outcomes and life chances of Arabic-speaking-background students in Years 9 and 10, who may have been in Australia for a number of years. The students are older and have had more opportunity to adjust to a primarily monolingual educational environment. In addition, the age of students in Years 9 and 10 suggests that there are other complicating factors affecting their educational achievements. At this age, teenagers are more cognitively aware of their social environment, their own identity and how they are situated within the wider public sphere. Such attitudinal and self-reflective factors mean that educational interventions need to be multi-tiered, rather than simply focused on linguistic factors. Thirdly, despite a number of isolated examples of successful bilingual education programs within the Australian educational system, bilingual education has not received widespread mainstream government policy and funding support. The current educational framework supported by the Australian Commonwealth and State governments emphasises, albeit at the normative level only, the development of multicultural (rather than bilingual) educational strategies. More broadly, engagement with the community and the real world is essential for engagement with school, and, therefore, there is an emphasis on developing skills and competencies beyond, though not to the exclusion of, literacy and numeracy.

Assumptions about Arab and Muslim Australians

Although debates about Muslim and Arab Australians' loyalty to their adopted country have thrived in a climate of fear and insecurity, there has been little research undertaken into the strategies used by members of this community to overcome increasingly racialised media and political discourses. One of the few such studies[2] examined the extent of social connectedness between Arab and Muslim Australians and the wider community, and the willingness of the former to engage beyond their own communities. It explored the ways in which assumptions about community-building through developing social capital might be more complex and problematic than policy-makers had anticipated. This, the study found, is particularly so in communities that are marginalised from contemporary Australian society. Public policy initiatives such as the Federal Government's 'Australians Working Together' initiative and the Victorian Government's 'Building Stronger Communities' focus on notions of community partnerships and 'social capital' as vehicles to promote social inclusion, wellbeing and connectedness by enhancing individual and community capacity. Such initiatives are based upon assumptions that social capital is essentially a positive attribute of individual and community engagement, that benefits all in equal measure, and that individuals have the capacity to access a wide range of social networks in Australian communities where diversity is readily accepted.

These assumptions, however, are being challenged in some quarters. First, ways of measuring social capital are complex, as the strength and range of social networks are highly dependent on variables such as education, gender and ethnicity. Arab communities place high value on 'bonding social capital', that is, the maintenance of family and kinship networks. However, many in recent years have migrated to Australia without those networks[3], and this brings with it a sense of social isolation and anxiety. In many instances, engagement in ethnic or religious organisations becomes an important part of replacing those networks and, in turn, establishing a sense of identity within the community. Involvement in inter-community organisations, however, can be a much more difficult proposition. One basic barrier can be a lack of language familiarity, but community attitudes that stigmatise and marginalise particular groups on the basis of assumed traits may also act as barriers to engagement in many forms of community participation. Groups that are marginalised through stigmatisation may consequently experience a narrowing of social networks, which exacerbates their social, educational and economic exclusion. Where family networks are also absent, adverse physical and mental health outcomes can result. Although few evaluations have been undertaken exploring the interface between diversity, anecdotal evidence[4] of community attitudes toward diversity, and the impacts of those attitudes on social connectedness for the groups concerned has indicated that such a scenario is occurring for members of Arabic and Muslim communities in Australia. Even less specific research has been undertaken into the ramifications of social, educational and economic marginalisation of Arabic and Muslim communities, most particularly Muslim women. This would appear to be due, at least in part, to the prevailing global events and their local ramifications as outlined earlier, which have resulted in the stereotyping of Arab and Muslim community members, not only in Australia but on a much larger scale.

The centrality of 'bonding social capital' in Arab and Muslim communities tends to ensure that they establish high levels of social cohesion and, in turn, this can be a source of social resilience. The more concerning area of potential social disconnectedness occurs where these groups experience relatively lower levels of engagement with the wider community, that is, 'bridging social capital'. This term refers to 'contacts between people of different backgrounds in terms of age, gender, ethnicity, education, socio-economic status and locality'.[5] Ideally, a balance between bonding social capital and bridging social capital will maintain and strengthen social connectedness. To understand a little better the importance of these two areas of social capital, we will explore them a little further. Bonding social capital is evident in a range of different forms. Ethnic heritage, for example, is a key element of collective identity and a major focus of networks and association. Religion is also significant as a form of bonding social capital and an important avenue for community participation and connection. Arab and Muslim Australians tend to live in close proximity to each other and this provides an essential source of mutual support. But even within these culturally bonded communities, such as those in outer north-west Melbourne where the *Diversity Project* conducted its research, the social climate became more difficult for Arabs and Muslims after September 2001. Lebanese-background students participating in a recent study into their motivational goals and school achievement in south-west Sydney[6] reported that they were treated differently from other members of the community when applying for work or accessing public services. They consequently suffered from a sense of being undervalued by the broader Australian community, and women, in particular, reported higher levels of discriminatory treatment. Despite a desire for closer interaction with the wider cross-cultural community, conflicts in the Middle East and the so-called 'war on terror' were believed to have exacerbated their sense of isolation. The assumption of certain traits based on race and ethnicity, largely derived from the media, erects barriers against active participation in the community for Arab and Muslim Australians. In a cruel irony this stigmatisation, and consequent marginalisation, then appears to confirm the prejudice that Arabs and Muslims do not integrate well. In turn, these groups naturally turn to the greater sense of security offered by the familiar links offered by 'bonding social capital' and shy away from the far less certain and uneasy realm of 'bridging social capital'.

External barriers to the promotion of bridging social capital, such as employer discrimination, limitations to inclusive educational opportunities or accessing culturally appropriate community services and resources are areas of concern to members of the Arab and Muslim communities. Hostility fuelled by racist and discriminatory depictions of Arabic and Islamic culture in the media are especially worrying. There are clear links between increasing problematisation of these groups and their increased experience of stress and lack of community safety and connectedness. Participants in the research project reported in this book and elsewhere[7] drew direct links between social exclusion, discrimination and disenfranchisement of Arab and Muslim Australians and their physical and mental health problems. This sense of exclusion is perhaps felt most acutely among young Muslim women who are often depicted as submissive and victimised by their religion, an image regularly exerted in the West.

The Student Demographic of the *Diversity Project*

The *Diversity Project* worked initially across schools in the north-west suburbs of Melbourne during the 2003–07 period. The schools included two coeducational and one all girls schools; however, the research focus reported in this book has been narrowed down to two schools—one coeducational and one girls' school—for the purposes of the longitudinal analysis presented here. The broader communities in which these two schools are located are quite different demographically. For example, the City of Hume, where the coeducational school is located, has a very high proportion of young people: currently, 32.5 per cent of the population is aged nineteen and younger.[8] Conversely, the City of Darebin, where the girls' school is situated has 'one of the largest populations of older people in the state'.[9] The demographic of the City of Hume reflects the broader patterns of Middle Eastern migration as represented in the 2005 ABS statistics, which found that Iraq was one of the three birth countries most rapidly on the increase in Australia. It was also among the youngest migrant groups in Australia.[10] This is indicative of a much more transient community where families tend to relocate more than once in the process of re-settlement. This was less the case in the suburb where the girls' school was situated, where families tend to be more permanently established. In both schools, however, a concentration of Iraqi students in Years 9 and 10 was evident. The *Diversity Project* sample, therefore, though small, represents a microcosm of the Arab and Muslim communities concentrated in pockets of Melbourne and Sydney and, as such, is an authentic representation of this group's experience.

There were twenty-nine coeducation students and thirty girls'-school students participating in the active research. All were from Years 9 and 10, and aged between fourteen and sixteen. Both of the schools represented high levels of cultural diversity and a significant percentage of overseas-born students: 58 per cent of the student population at the coeducational school was born in thirty different countries and 47 per cent of the girls' school in thirty-six different countries. In the coeducational school, 38 per cent of overseas-born students were from Iraq and 44 per cent of them were in Years 9 and 10 at the time the research was undertaken. At the girls' school, students born in Iraq represented the highest percentage of any nationality (11 per cent) and just over half of these students (54 per cent) were enrolled in Years 9 and 10. The birth place of the Years 9 and 10 cohorts at each of the schools is represented in Figure 1. As the graph demonstrates, almost twice as many students were born in Iraq at the coeducational school as at the girls' school. They accounted for 68 per cent of those surveyed, and the majority of them (78 per cent) had arrived in Australia within the last five years. At the girls' school, just over half were born overseas, 58 per cent of whom had arrived in Australia within the last five years. The percentage of recent arrivals among each group suggests that a majority of them have had a disrupted education for one or more reasons: through the various

Identity, Education and Belonging

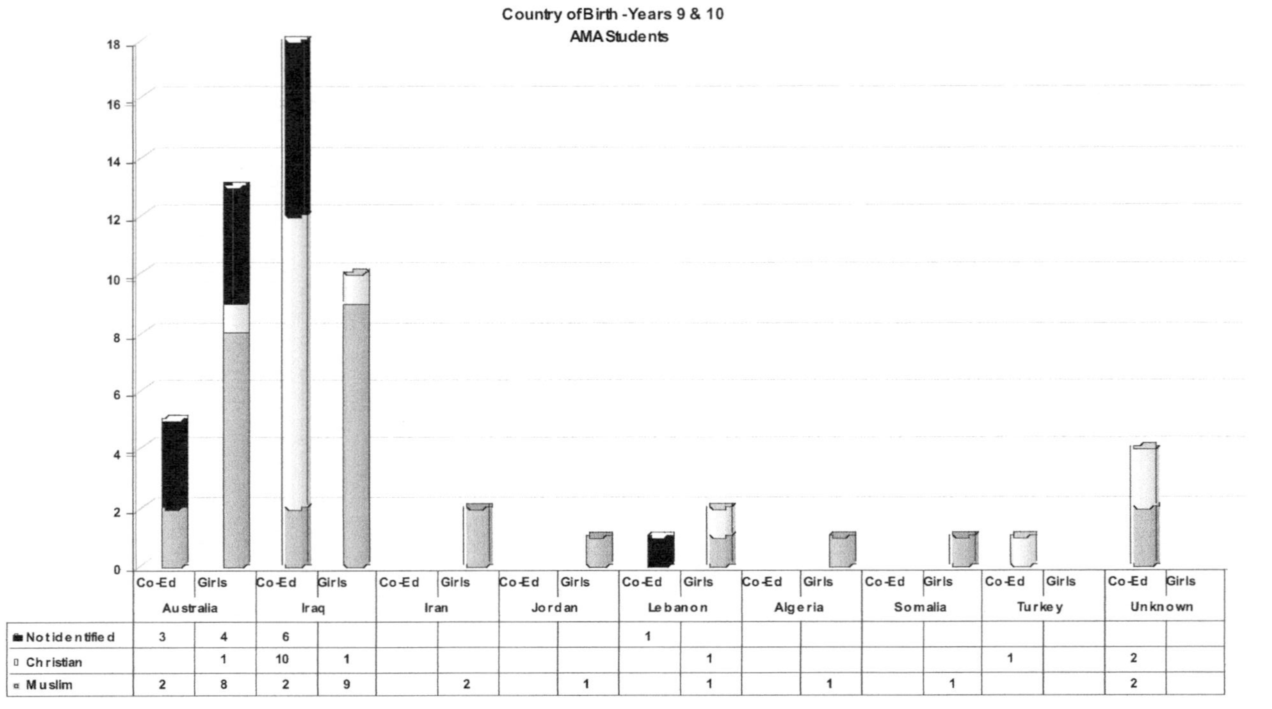

	Australia		Iraq		Iran		Jordan		Lebanon		Algeria		Somalia		Turkey		Unknown	
	Co-Ed	Girls	Co-Ed	Girls	Co-Ed	Girls	Co-Ed	Girls	Co-Ed	Girls	Co-Ed	Girls	Co-Ed	Girls	Co-Ed	Girls	Co-Ed	Girls
Not identified	3	4	6						1									
Christian		1	10	1						1					1		2	
Muslim	2	8	2	9		2		1		1		1		1			2	

Figure 1: Students' Country of Birth

transitional phases of migration, internal movement since arrival in Australia and, in some instances, detention in refugee camps. Any, or a combination of all, of these circumstances has resulted in a lack of experience or continuity in English-language education.

In terms of language representation in the two schools, 67 per cent of the entire coeducational student population came from a Language Background Other Than English (LBOTE) and of this group 27 per cent nominated Assyrian as their first language; 16 per cent Arabic; and 13 per cent Turkish. Looking at only the Year 9 and 10 students in the coeducational school, a huge majority of 91 per cent and 90 per cent respectively spoke a language other than English at home. In the majority of instances (73 per cent) these were languages of Middle Eastern origin: 48 per cent of these spoke Assyrian, 27 per cent Arabic, 20 per cent Turkish, 3 per cent Persian and 2 per cent Hebrew. In the girls' school, 55 per cent of the entire student population was from a LBOTE background, a third of whom (30 per cent) spoke Arabic at home. Taking into consideration only the Year 9 and 10 students, 40 per cent spoke a Middle Eastern language: 85 per cent of these spoke Arabic, 8 per cent Persian, 4 per cent Assyrian and 3 per cent Turkish. With only 1.2 per cent of the Australian population speaking Arabic at home according to the 2006 Census, this is an indication of the significant concentration of Arabic-speaking families in some areas of Sydney and Melbourne.

The religious representation among the Year 9 and 10 cohorts typically defied assumptions about the Arab and Muslim Australian youth population. Although almost half of the boys completing the *Diversity Project* survey did not respond to the question about religion, 48 per cent nominated Christianity. However, the high number of Assyrian speakers among the group, which denotes a Christian affiliation, makes it safe to assume a comfortable majority of Christians among the coeducational students. At the girls' school, only 13 per cent chose not to divulge their religion and of those who did a majority of 77 per cent were Muslim and 10 per cent Christian. As well as marking the different demographic cohorts across the two schools, this also provides some clues as to gender sensitivities among Arab and Muslim families. The higher concentration of Muslims among the girls'-school cohort is itself indicative of parents' preference that their daughters attend a single sex, rather than a

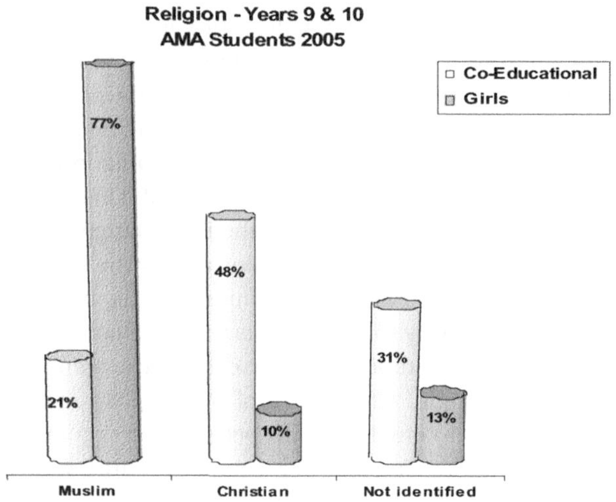

Figure 2: Students' Religion

coeducational, school. In fact, students attending the girls' school in many instances come from a wide radius of suburbs, some quite distant, underscoring this point. That many of the girls'-school families travel some distance each day means that they have little investment of identity in the community in which their daughters' school is located. Students at the coeducational school, however, have an investment of identity in the community in which their school is located, and as a young community, keenly feel the negative representations of Arabs and Muslims. For example, the coeducational school is situated in the heart of a community in which some arrests of 'terror suspects' were made in 2005. The media focus upon the area resulted in defensiveness among some of the boys during focus-group discussions, and one wrote on the survey: 'I don't like this survey because it is trying to say Arabs are different from the world, that's why youse [sic] are doing this.'

Yet, as Figure 2 reveals, the majority of students surveyed at the coeducational school were not Muslim but Christian. This confirms the point that Arab and Muslim identity has been incorrectly conflated in the public imagination. What might have been presumed to be homogenous pockets of Muslims and/or Arabs instead represents a diversity of religion, ethnicity and culture, which marks these communities as typically multicultural. As such, each student cohort represents the tension between complex and simplified identity formations that find many young people, born in Australia of overseas-born parents, choosing to retain 'hyphenated' identities, often depending upon the circumstances in which they find themselves. That is, they maintain strong ethnic, linguistic and cultural affiliations that often fluctuate between their public and private worlds. For example, several students in focus groups vacillated between thinking of themselves as 'Lebbo' in some circumstances, and Australian in others. However, within this sense of indecision, which moved between the private (home) and public (school) spaces, they felt themselves to be part of a subset of 'wogs'. The question of what was meant by the term prompted the following exchange among the coeducational students who lived in the more socio-economically depressed area:

> Facilitator: You keep using the word 'wog'. I'm interested where a wog comes from.
>
> Female Student (FS): To me there's different kinds of wogs. Like, pure wogs are Syrians, Iraqis, Lebbos.
>
> Male Student (MS): Arabs.
>
> FS: Yeah, Arabs. Then there's Greeks, Italians, and all those wogs.
>
> Facilitator: And is being a wog a bad thing?
>
> FS: No, it's a good thing.
>
> Facilitator: Why is it a good thing?
>
> FS: 'Cos I don't want to be an Aussie.
>
> Facilitator: What puts you off the thought of being Australian?
>
> FS: 'Cos most of them, they just drink and they get fat.

While the group thought this comment was funny, it did reflect attitudes towards Australians that are as bound up in stereotypes as some of the dominant culture's narrow perceptions of Arabs and Muslims. But it also reflected some deeper anxieties about what it might mean to embrace a purely 'Australian' identity that might mean losing touch with the family's religion, culture of origin and moral framework. This was evident when the discussion moved on to observations of Australians in their neighbourhood. The tone of the discussion became much more serious, but it was also evident that the students idealised their own culture for the sense of security it offered:

> MS: In our country, you know like our religion, Arabs, there's no, like, rows or anything. If anyone argues with their parents, they don't get kicked out of the house.

> FS: Aussies get kicked out and that.

> MS: I saw this girl, I was talking to her in the street. My friend was asking her what are you doing? She's like, 'I got kicked out of the house.'

> FS: Like if I've done something bad, my dad would probably hit us. Or if not hit, he would yell. But he would never kick me out. Like, even if I tried to get out.

> Facilitator: What's worse, being kicked out or being hit?

> FS: Being kicked out. I don't want to get out of my home. Also because they end up with no job, they end up junkies.

> MS: Smoking choof.

> FS: Having babies. My neighbour, she's got a baby. She's only sixteen years old. She's onto her second.

> Facilitator: Is she what you'd call an Aussie?

> FS: Yeah, she is. Her mum lives with her. She's got, like, in and out guys in the house.

> MS: That's like in my street. Everyone's Aussie and everyone takes drugs, they smoke choof.

Facilitator: What do you think the difference is here? Why do you think Aussies do whatever they like?

FS: Because we have respect for our parents. Like, we don't act up, we don't swear. And if we do, we get hit and we learn our lesson. We don't get kicked out.

FS: Miss, Aussies, their parents let them go out till any time. Like, I would love to go to more places, like shopping, but I'm hardly allowed to go. But Aussies, they can go to the city, clubbing.

MS: I've seen some Aussies, they swear to their mum. I think, how could they swear to their parents? I would never swear to my parents. Most of the ones I know, they all have like step-dads and step-mums.

FS: Yeah, like in our backgrounds, like Arab, it's not good for us to get divorced. For Aussies, they don't care. Like they can get divorced, get another husband. For us it's not good.

Through this range of concerns among a Year 9 group—from drugs to discipline, teenage sexuality to divorce—the pressure of adaptation and belonging became much clearer. The fears that some students and parents have about surrendering their identities to embrace 'Australianness' was perhaps even more acutely drawn from a Year 10 girl of Lebanese-Australian background who candidly acknowledged that: '… with my family, my mum thinks that school is actually corrupting me because when I go home I don't speak like Arabic and that. And she wants me to speak full Arabic. And she always says that school's corrupting me. And she always wants me to go to Arabic school to learn Arabic.'

The tensions between the private and public worlds of some Arab and Muslim students is, of course, heightened and more confusing still when external community pressures are exacerbated by the media, such as in the aftermath of September 11. The internal pressures to adhere to time-honoured cultural, linguistic and religious identities are intensified and the compulsion to retreat into that secure space more persuasive. This is made more difficult for the children of parents, such as this Year 10 girl's mother, who might have had very limited experience of education in a secular Australian school. Some parents have had no experience of education in their country of origin either and so their expectations of what school means for their children does not correlate with their child's. (The experience of Arab and Muslim parents is discussed in the next chapter.) This pressure between the private and public worlds of young Arab and Muslim students can make the prospect of identification as Australians troubling, but in other ways reassuring.

Citizenship, Identity and Belonging among Arab and Muslim Australian Students

Citizenship can signify an important foundation by conferring a sense of belonging that can override the competing, sometimes conflicting, demands upon a young person's loyalties. For those who have fled sites of conflict with their families, citizenship in their country of settlement can offer a degree of personal security and freedom from blame for the activities undertaken by extremists in their country of origin. For Arab and Muslim youth, whether first-, second- or third-generation Australians, citizenship forms an important part of their self-perception as Australians. The ideas of citizenship are introduced to secondary-school students by the Federal Government's *Discovering Democracy* curriculum, which introduces them to citizenship as a primary source of identity, largely framed within the current discourse of 'values'. Citizenship is extended to those who accept a series of conditions based on 'the essential values of Australian society' including respect for the law; freedom of religion; respect for people from other cultures; and the understanding that people do not have the right to encourage violence or racial hatred.[11] As the research among Arab and Muslim secondary-school students in the study found, students, on the one hand, understand the contract they have entered into as new Australian citizens, but on the other, they are often perplexed that non-Muslim Australians transgress this implicit pact as fellow citizens. This was most acutely felt at the time of September 11, which was seen as an attack on the West generally, when even primary-school students were vilified for simply being Muslim as reported by one student: '… after 9/11, you know what happened in America, they all used to say to me "she's got a bomb in her pencil case, she's going to bomb the school", just 'cos I was a Muslim'.

Since then, a sense of confusion and alienation on several levels has become increasingly acute for many Arab and Muslim youth and makes the conceptualisation of 'Muslim youth in Australia'—an idea built on a generalisation—more problematic. The first, and perhaps most fundamental over-simplification of identity attributed to Muslims, as outlined earlier, relates to gender. Additionally, a range of presuppositions about Muslims in Australia adds further layers of misconception: that Muslims share one culture; that they all speak Arabic; that people from the Middle East are all Arabs or that they form one 'race'. Add to this the assumption that Muslims are anti-secular, zealous or trapped in tradition. These confused stereotypes are especially perplexing for young people whose families are of Arab and/or Muslim background but who want to identify themselves as Australian, without revoking their cultural heritage, in much the same way as an Australian of Irish ancestry might continue to identify with that culture of origin some generations after settlement. The sense of frustration experienced by young Arab and Muslim Australians surfaces when the media exploits issues involving these groups:

> … we're silenced, the wrong stuff is said about us, people are going against us, we feel guilty, we feel alienated, we thought that we were Australians, we've been taught that this is a multicultural country for everybody and we should feel a part of it. Now we're feeling less a part of it, unfortunately.[12]

Muslims living in Australia, especially those born here, struggle to conceptualise themselves as one group. 'There is no such thing as a representative Muslim voice which speaks for all Australian Muslims' one participant said in an ABC report on 'Australian Muslim Youth'.[13] This, in itself, creates enormous confusion for young Muslims who feel powerless to rectify misunderstandings about their religion, and wonder why, when Australia is celebrated as a multicultural society, they are compelled to justify themselves. The struggle to claim an identity, however, is not just imposed externally. Some young Muslims feel that the older generation which has not grown up in, and been shaped by, Australian society does not understand what it means to be a young Australian Muslim either. Irfan Yusuf, a Sydney lawyer and columnist, commented:

> If you look at the people that the government is currently talking to [referring to the Prime Minister's Muslim Summit in 2005], they're not really representative of Muslim reality, and a lot of these leaders, I don't know, maybe think we're not orthodox enough, or maybe they think we don't fit their mould of what a Muslim should be, because I guess a lot of them think that they expect a Muslim to have a migrant background, or a lot of them are very reluctant to pass on the mantle to the next generation.[14]

When John Howard publicly remarked in September 2006 that Muslims in Australia must learn English, embrace Australian values and treat their women equally, responses from the Muslim community underscored this point. The then–Chairman of the Prime Minister's Muslim Reference Group suggested that another riot such as Cronulla might take place if Muslims are continually singled out in this way. However, one younger Muslim agreed with the former prime minister, recognising that young people often reflect the desire of their parents to resist integration due to fears of moral laxity, a position that can undermine their position in the community. Of course, it is questionable whether equating integration with certain social behaviours is a legitimate basis for undermining the Muslim community's place within the wider mainstream society.[15] But young Muslims are more likely to be socially shaped by the mainstream society, and so will inevitably have to learn to live across the 'old world' that their family left behind and the 'new world' in which they now live.

Islamic leadership in Australia has been dominated by community members who were not born, educated or socialised in Australia, and this has posed problems for young Muslims looking for guidance that is responsive to their experience. The fact that the Howard Government's Muslim Advisory Board was dominated by Muslims with religious affiliations also underscored this. The board—and the

Council for Multiculturalism in Australia—was dismantled when its term ended in 2006. The new Rudd Government is seeking to re-establish both, and by engaging Muslims from across the community rather than focusing on spiritual leaders, it is hoped that the new organisation will help to 'dismantle the stereotypical picture of Islam'.[16] But still, there remains no capacity yet for training Islamic religious leaders in Australia, the imams to whom the Muslim community turns for spiritual guidance here are 'imported' and this 'creates a gulf between the born Muslim population and the second generation Muslims'.[17] Young Muslims can, therefore, find themselves caught in a double bind: though strongly identifying with their religious heritage, they are unsure that they are accurately represented from within their own community. School is often the one area in which young people are able to consolidate their sense of identity and belonging, simply because either their friends share a similar cultural and social experience, or are similarly from 'non-Anglo' backgrounds. Indeed, the students participating in the *Diversity Project* were asked about their friendships across ethnic groups at school and about ethnic relations at school more generally. At the coeducational school, where the students lived in close proximity to the school, there were much higher levels of interaction among ethnic groups: 66 per cent said that they had 'a wide range' of friends from different ethnic groups. This was not, however, the case at the girls'

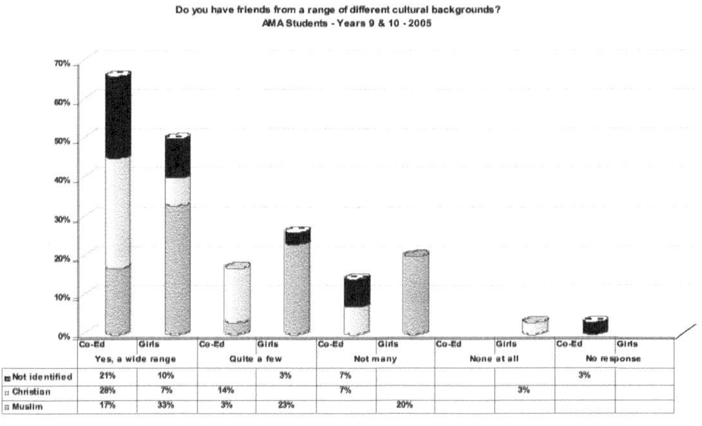

	Yes, a wide range		Quite a few		Not many		None at all		No response	
	Co-Ed	Girls	Co-Ed	Girls	Co-Ed	Girls	Co-Ed	Girls	Co-Ed	Girls
Not identified	21%	10%		3%	7%				3%	
Christian	28%	7%	14%		7%			3%		
Muslim	17%	33%	3%	23%		20%				

Figure 3: Students' Friendships at School

school. Here, only 50 per cent had 'a wide range of friends' across ethnic groups as Figure 3 reflects.

Possible reasons for this difference are twofold. First, students from the girls' school travel, in several cases, some distance each day to school and are, therefore, not bonded with the local community from which the wider school population is drawn. In such circumstances, it is a natural inclination to gravitate towards familiarity. Second, there was a high number of students at the girls' school whose Islamic faith was more visible through their wearing hijab to school, which again enforced a sense of connection with girls of the same background. The broader question regarding school-wide relationships among ethnic groups yielded a similar difference. The vast majority of coeducation students (93 per cent) thought that relations between ethnic groups at school were either 'good' (72 per cent) or 'excellent' (21 per cent). Again, wider neighbourhood connections might account for this as students living within walking distance from the school interact beyond their tight-knit school groups when moving to and from school. This seems to be confirmed by the fact that only 66 per cent at the girls' school believed that relations were either 'good' (46 per cent) or 'excellent' (20 per cent), and one third (33 per cent) thought ethnic relations at school were only average. Many of these girls travel to and from school by car and so have very limited interactions with their Year 9 or 10 peers beyond the school

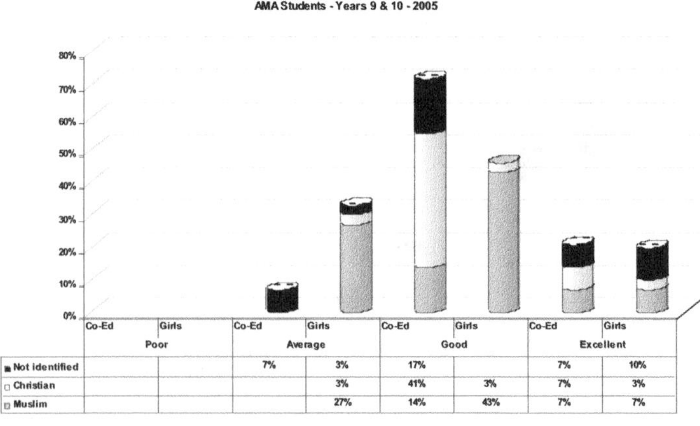

	Poor		Average		Good		Excellent	
	Co-Ed	Girls	Co-Ed	Girls	Co-Ed	Girls	Co-Ed	Girls
Not identified			7%	3%	17%		7%	10%
Christian				3%	41%	3%	7%	3%
Muslim				27%	14%	43%	7%	7%

Figure 4: Ethnic Relations at School

gate. As already mentioned, many of these girls also wear the hijab and tend to stick together through a strong mutual identification.

These findings among a microcosm of Arab and Muslim youth in north-west Melbourne reflect the broader issues around gender and Islam that were discussed earlier. Girls from both schools reported instances of public humiliation because of either wearing the hijab themselves, or being with an older woman wearing the veil. This sense of vulnerability cuts to the core of young Arab and Muslim girls' sense of belonging and trust, as one girl explained during a focus-group discussion:

> I feel like I'm an Australian but I don't know. Like, some Australian people, if they find out I'm Lebanese, you know, they kind of treat me differently. And it's like, once I was in a shop and there was this Aussie person in there and she said 'go back to your country' and all this stuff. And once I saw a lady that was in a scarf and there was a lady at the cash register treating her different to all the other customers. I find that, I don't know. That's why sometimes I feel like I'm not Australian, because of that.

The issue of self-perception among Arab and Muslim young people beyond the school environment, and how community perceptions of gender in Islam impact upon them, is explored further in the next chapter. Here we wish to delve further into the school experience of Arab and Muslim students to find out what their ambitions for the future are, and whether the *Diversity Project* affirmed, or dispelled, perceptions about this group's achievements and aspirations in secondary school.

Arab and Muslim Australian Students' Educational Experiences

School is, of course, a relatively fleeting experience in an individual's life. It is therefore critical to capture that opportunity to nurture a secure sense of self on several levels. The *Diversity Project* found that secondary schools, as a comparatively neutral environment, can provide an optimal degree of flexibility within current curricular, pedagogical, administrative and socio-cultural frameworks. As set out in the *Adelaide Declaration* discussed earlier, one of the vital purposes of education is to ensure that all students, irrespective of race, gender or religious background, benefit from learning in ways that facilitate their full participation in public, community and economic life. As we discussed in the previous chapter, studies of Arab-Australian youth undertaken in the 1980s and 1990s found that they were less confident in their abilities to achieve education or training beyond secondary school, and were more likely to hold more limited educational ambitions than students from other cultural backgrounds. While these students tended to think that their parents considered education to be of importance, many of them were less likely to discuss their education with their parents.

The *Diversity Project* found very similar levels of confidence that school could help them pursue their future ambitions among students surveyed across both schools. A total of 69 per cent of coeducational students and 67 per cent of girls'-school participants responded 'yes, definitely' when asked this question. The majority of students surveyed did appear to be genuinely positive about school and their future. This girl's comment is a reflection of this positive attitude towards education: 'I really do enjoy school. Learning to me is very valuable and since I am doing well I would like to continue my learning and finish university.'

A total of 90 per cent of participants at the girls' school, compared to 80 per cent at the coeducational school, indicated that they definitely wanted to go to university or TAFE. Given the number of relatively newly arrived students among the coeducational cohort some, like this student, felt 'frustrated because I like to achieve but I am not able to [with] my level of English language'. Despite the challenges of language and re-settlement, however, there was an overall optimism about the future. Importantly, no student chose the response 'I don't care', leaving an impression that, at least among this sampling of attitudes, Arab and Muslim students were resolute about finishing school. This confirms other studies' findings (discussed in Chapter 2) that migrant families often have high educational aspirations for their children, even when these are not necessarily matched to their child's ability to achieve those ambitions due to, for example, linguistic barriers or disrupted educational continuity. It also debunks some of the myths around gender in Islamic communities, with girls demonstrating high levels of motivation to complete secondary school and go on to tertiary studies and careers. This point was explored further in focus-group discussions when students were asked about their, and their parents', ambitions for them. Their comments suggested that Muslim families, like any other in society, hold similar aspirations for their sons as well as their daughters, as two girls stated: 'My mum wants me to work first and then she wants me to get married and have a family.' 'My father wants me to be something good because he never got to be. He wants me to be better than him.'

The focus-group discussions did dispel many myths around gender in Islam. Although there was one participant in the girls' school who was, at the age of sixteen, already betrothed to a boy in Algeria—and one such case was reported at the coeducational school, though this student was not connected with the research—the families of girls in both schools appeared to have equal aspirations for their male and female children. When asked 'Do you find in your families, those who have brothers, your parents are equally supportive of brothers and sisters?' one student from the girls' school went so far as to say that her parents were more academically ambitious for the sisters in the family. Other girls in the group nodded in agreement, that their parents actually encouraged them more than their brothers to strive and do well at school. It might be that these students' responses were defensive against the gender stereotypes propagated by the media, or the fact that they were at an all-girls' school reinforced the importance of education for girls. It would, of course, be simplistic to draw too many conclusions from these responses within such a small study; however, it does take us some way towards exposing the generalisations propagated in the media, particularly in such cases as the 'Brides of Islam' story discussed earlier, published in *The Australian*.

These broader social concerns aside, the *Diversity Project* found that school was clearly an important site of belonging and inclusion among both groups of Arab and Muslim students. This was affirmed in the surveys which asked students to nominate the words that best described their experience of school. Boys and girls, whether overseas- or Australian-born, overwhelmingly chose the words 'caring' and 'friendly' to describe school, reflecting its importance as a place of wellbeing when the broader community could often appear perplexing. Their responses also confirm the point discussed earlier, that though some Arab and Muslim Australian students might experience hostility in the wider community, particularly at times when external events have aroused public fear, school is a site of stability and continuity.

As we stated at the outset, the *Diversity Project* was distinguished from earlier studies into Arab and Muslim social groups by its focus on the interconnecting experiences of students, parents and teachers. It was believed that a study into educational diversity approached from this range of perspectives was timely, in an era infused with fears about terrorism, and when the concept of multiculturalism appears to be receding from public life amid suspicions that it has failed. Citizenship and its requisites, as discussed earlier, link closely with perceptions of identity and belonging, both of which are central to understanding the experiences of Arab and Muslim Australian students in Australia. We now turn our focus to the broader influences in the school setting—what the *Diversity Project* called the 'Four P' approach: Policy, Parents, Professional Development and Practice. As this suggests, we focus on the nature of students' community engagement as part of their extra-curricular activities. In this section we will also contrast their experiences with those of non-Arab and non-Muslim students to gauge any slippage between these two groups. We also look with more detail into Arab and Muslim parents' engagement with the schools to understand what impact this has on their children's educational achievement and sense of belonging. We then discuss how these elements can be drawn together to positively influence teacher professional practice and the overall dynamic of school communities.

Notes

1   Suliman & McInerney.
2   S Kenny, F Mansouri and P Spratt, 2005, *Arabic Communities and Well-Being: Supports and Barriers to Social Connectedness*, Centre For Citizenship & Human Rights (CCHR), Deakin University, Geelong.
3   ibid., p. 61.
4   ibid.
5   V Jochum, 2003, 'Social Capital: Beyond the Theory', National Council for Voluntary Organisations (NCVO), London, p. 10.

6   Suliman and McInerney.

7   ibid.

8   *Our Profile—Hume City of Today*, City of Hume, www.hume.vic.gov.au, viewed 7 July 2008.

9   *Community and Diversity Profile*, City of Darebin, www.cityofdarebin. vic.gov.au, viewed 7 July 2008.

10   *Muslims in Australia—A Snapshot*, 2007, Department of Immigration and Citizenship, http://www.immi.gov.au/media/publications/ multicultural/pdf_doc/Muslims_in_Australia_snapshot.pdf, viewed 18 June 2007

11   From *Discovering Democracy*, 'What Sort of Nation?' Focus question 2: How has Immigration Shaped the Kind of Nation We Are? Teaching and Learning Activities – Activity 7: Conditions of Citizenship, p. 14, www. curriculum.edu.au/ddunits/units/ms5fq2acts.htm#Activity%207, viewed 18 June 2007.

12   Belad Assad, 2005, teacher at Werribee Islamic College, speaking in Tom Morton's 'Australian Muslim Youth', *Background Briefing*, ABC Radio National, 11 December. www.abc.net.au/rn/backgroundbriefing/ stories/2005/1526049.htm.

13   ibid.

14   ibid.

15   See Stephen Crittenden's discussion with Chairman of the Muslim Reference Group, Dr Ameer Ali and Sydney psychiatrist, Dr Tanveer Ahmed, on the *Religion Report*, ABC Radio National, 6 September 2006, www.abc.net.au/rn/religionreport/stories/2006/1733620.htm.

16   Richard Kerbaj, 2008, 'Rudd's Quest for True Blue Muslims', *The Australian*, 11 March.

17   Bilal Cleland, 2001, 'Spreading the Message of Islam in Anglo-Australia: Developing a Positive Image for Islam in Australia'. Part 2 of a lecture presented on 3 March at Curtin University, Perth. Organised by FAMSY (WA) and CMSA (Curtin University MSA) and printed in *Salam Magazine*, www.famsy.com/salam/IslamOz61.htm, viewed 1 June 2006.

Chapter 4

A Partnership Approach to Diversity in Education

This chapter investigates the deployment of a model that takes a multidimensional approach to the education of high-school children from Arab and Muslim backgrounds. The model was primarily aimed at improving the educational outcomes of Arab and Muslim secondary-school students in the crucial Years 9 and 10 when students are at greatest risk of disengaging from school. The model attempts to move away from a construction of education that posits students as passive receivers of information delivered by neutrally positioned teachers. Such an approach aims to affirm that both recognising and understanding cultural difference can challenge the barriers that prevent minority groups from accessing particular social goods, and society at large. By developing students' sense of their various cultural identities, the model aims to give them the skills and knowledge necessary to access the mainstream culture as well as other cultures. It therefore promotes transformation across those areas that contribute to social, institutional and educational disadvantages often found alongside cultural difference.

If the entire school is engaged in a process of collaborative negotiation of structural and pedagogical adjustment, then students arc likely to find school changes more meaningful, rich and consistent. Moreover, the partnership approach underpinning the project recognised the skills and intelligence that students bring to a participatory educational dialogue. While there may be an emphasis on promoting improved learning outcomes for those students who often experience educational disadvantage, there are some concrete ways to establish the argument that the benefits of an inclusive multicultural education extends beyond these students and their immediate schools. This model, therefore, suggests that recognising a school's multicultural context in the delivery of equitable education is of benefit to all involved in the educational process, not only minority students.

When the *Diversity Project* started in its current multidimensional form in 2003–2004, the preliminary research findings suggested that Arab and Muslim Australian students exhibited negative tendencies in key areas relating to teacher–student relations, perceptions of inter-ethnic relations at school, confidence in achieving a tertiary place, beliefs about whether racism affects learning and behaviour, and family emphasis upon and attitudes towards education. More worrying perhaps was the fact that Arab and Muslim Australian students were more likely to express distrust towards teachers, particularly based on a perceived lack of cultural understanding. They were less confident in their abilities to achieve education or training beyond secondary school and were more likely to hold more limited educational ambitions than students from other backgrounds. While all students tended to think that their parents regarded education to be of importance, Arab and Muslim Australian students were less likely to discuss their education with their parents.

The *Diversity Project's* multidimensional approach was innovative in its engagement with all stakeholders in education—the students, their parents, and the teachers—and to achieve this, a 'cultural diversity facilitator' was appointed. This proved fundamental to the success of engaging and connecting the student, parent, staff and teacher groups within a partnership model that aims to be transformative in ensuring equitable access to quality education for all. The 'transformative multidimensional' model therefore recognised the interdependent nature of the learning experience and the critical role of social and cultural factors in shaping the educational achievements of Arab and Muslim Australian students, and CALD students more generally. Its findings confirmed the basic principle that the comparatively lower achievements of Arab and Muslim students reflected their attitudes towards their social and cultural environment and their parents' understanding of schooling policies and attitudes towards education achievements. In order to address negative trends, the *Diversity Project* developed intervention strategies that would be sustainable and complementary to existing educational and structural resources. The research and evaluation undertaken in the participating schools clearly shows that significant and measurable improvement in students' attitudes towards schools, teachers and their surrounding communities is possible. The positive attitudinal change detected among Year 9 and 10 students has taken place within an integrated action plan that involved parental engagement; case management performed systematically through the cultural diversity facilitator; and teachers' professional development (PD) sessions and community liaison. These attitudinal, cultural and societal shifts have contributed to improve educational outcomes, as reported by the schools independently.

Through quantitative and qualitative analysis of identity, cultural, attitudinal and structural factors that impact upon educational access, the *Diversity Project* first endeavoured to understand students' social attitudes and educational experiences. It then moved towards positive change through engaging Arab and Muslim parents, and curricular and pedagogical transformation that focused on student experience. In this way, it established links across these three stakeholders—students, parents, teachers and staff—by taking into consideration their unique perspectives. A microcosm of the wider community was thus recognised within the school community, a template that is present in all schools as a reflection of its wider socio-educational setting. The *Diversity Project* reflects recent research that has found that there are many dimensions to achieving successful multicultural education.[1] What distinguishes this study, however, is its multidimensional framework that highlights a range of heuristic factors and structural attributes that can determine the nature of a school's inter-ethnic relations, on-the-ground resources and skills available, and its wider socio-economic and socio-cultural setting. In particular, the *Diversity Project* explored the particular cultural, attitudinal, identity and structural dimensions that most affect the needs of Arab and Muslim students, and how such dimensions can be approached by schools to optimise their educational experiences and outcomes. Through focus groups, interviews and surveys with students (of both Arab-Muslim and non-Arab-Muslim backgrounds), parents and teachers, the study explored these dimensions of multicultural education.

Student Community Engagement

The first strategy in this approach focused on students. As well as the ongoing surveys and focus-group discussions with Year 9 and 10 students at the schools, creative outlets aimed at developing a forum for cultural expression were developed. For example, the Anti-Racism Action Band (A.R.A.B.), a Victorian Arabic Social Services (VASS) initiative, has been a hugely popular creative outlet for students who have also performed at several community events with the group. A.R.A.B. combines hip-hop, belly dance, rap and Derbakki (Arabic drumming), carries with it a message about self-esteem and inclusiveness, but most of all, the message that dance transcends race. The ongoing nature of the A.R.A.B. initiative has become a part of the extra-curricular life of some schools, as have programs organised by other NGOs, such as the Lebanese Welfare Society's rap dance classes, which establish an ongoing contribution to the cultural dynamic of schools. Other cultural activities on the school calendar, however, are more spasmodic and, therefore, less likely to contribute to long-term, structural transformation. The former Federal Government's annual Harmony Day program, for example, encouraged students to reflect on and express their intercultural identities for a day, but tended towards tokenism by addressing culture as a form of folkloric entertainment. The Harmony Day program was under review at the time of writing, as the new Rudd Government looked to 'develop a fresh approach for bringing Australians of all backgrounds together in a positive and productive way'.[2]

Constructive student interaction with the community now forms a part of the Victorian school curriculum since the implementation of VELS (Victorian Education Learning Standards) in 2006. VELS recognises that students, particularly those in Years 9 and 10, need to engage with the community in order to make their educational experience relevant to their futures. This provides an opportunity for the school to develop resources, in collaboration with a designated cultural-diversity facilitator, in ways that are relevant to the school community while also being responsive to curriculum requirements. As well as NGOs, city councils and the police force have also played an important part in creating opportunities for students to participate in community activities. For example, Arab and Muslim students were invited by one city council to hear a member of the Revolutionary Association of the Women of Afghanistan (RAWA) speak about the plight of Afghan women. On another occasion, the A.R.A.B. group performed at a Youth Safety Forum hosted by the Victoria Police. These initiatives empower students to actively participate in community events and broaden their social perspectives. This type of extra-currcular activity, encouraging deeper community engagement, was central to the *Diversity Project*'s objectives. In 2006, however, the study found that Arab and Muslim students were still less inclined to get involved in community activities at school. Only half of the coeducational Arab and Muslim students surveyed (54 per cent) were either 'regularly' (24 per cent) or 'sometimes' (30 per cent) involved in extra-curricular activities, compared to 69 per cent of the non-Arab and non-Muslim students. In addition, the latter group were involved in a much wider range of activities which included leadership training, peer support and initiatives such as anti-bullying and P.E.A.C.E. groups. Arab and Muslim students, as indicated in Figure 5, were most interested in sports, and these other activities were taken up by only small numbers.

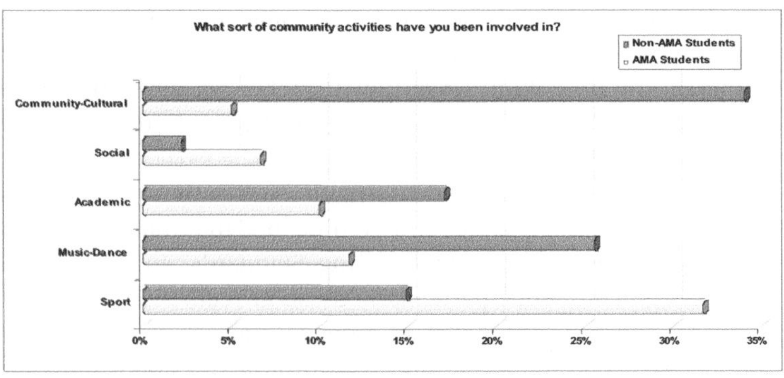

Figure 5: Student Engagement in Community Activities

Nevertheless students across both groups were keen to see more community activities at school. Again, the most popular for Arab and Muslim students was sport, followed by dance, while other students wanted more music activities and camps. School camps, it was noted, were not generally favoured by Arab and Muslim families. Discussions with the schools' student-welfare coordinators revealed that the reasons for this were twofold. First, several of these recently arrived families had experienced trauma and anxiety before settling in Australia and were reluctant to stray much beyond their familiar communities. Second, they often had insufficient levels of experience in their school community, or understanding of the purpose of school camps, to feel confident about their children attending. These sentiments were generally shared by both parents and students. This finding in the *Diversity Project* research, both quantitative and qualitative, reaffirmed the importance of community engagement among Arab and Muslim families as a means of 'bonding social capital', that is, the maintenance of cultural and religious networks, especially where wider family bonds might have been severed through migration. The importance of the study's findings lies in the recognition that this 'bonding social capital' needed to be extended to the school community also, as a priority for students *and* their parents. In this respect the *Diversity Project* pre-empted the Rudd Government's recognition that the involvement of parents in community activities—in this instance, in their children's school—was a vital link to a more meaningful sense of belonging that would benefit both students and parents. Parents and their involvement in and contribution to their children's schooling were, therefore, the second imperative of the *Diversity Project.*

The Parent Demographic of the *Diversity Project*

Increased parental attendance at school events, a more proactive attitude towards their children's education, and their willingness to form permanent parent–teacher forums were all indicators of positive change. This was achieved not only in the participating parents' increased confidence when engaging with the school, but was also reflected in their children's increased interaction with their family/parents regarding their education. A central part of this shift was made possible by the role played by the cultural-diversity facilitator who worked systematically towards bridging the communication and cultural gap between the schools and the parents/communities. The positive views expressed by the students and parents regarding this community-based approach reaffirmed the importance of bridging this gap, particularly in communities that face considerable economic, linguistic and social obstacles, such as was the case in the *Diversity Project's* partnership schools. The number of parents engaged in the active research increased steadily over three years (2004 to 2006) as the facilitator's presence became more firmly established. For the purposes of establishing a profile of the parents engaged in the study over those three years, we combine all seventy-eight of them (forty-five women and thirty-three men), 63 per cent of whom were aged in their forties and fifties. It is important to note that parent participants were drawn from the entire Arab and Muslim school community, rather than specifically the parents of the Year 9 and 10 students involved. We, therefore, see some differential in the country-of-origin data, with a higher proportion of Lebanese families represented than was indicated among students. Nevertheless, parents of Iraqi origin are still easily predominant as illustrated in Figure 6 below.

It is also quite noticeable in this graph that there was a much higher number of Christian parents who volunteered to participate in focus-group discussions and information sessions organised by the

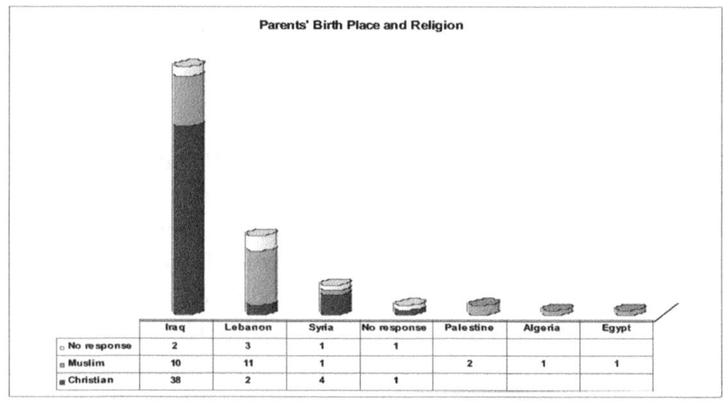

	Iraq	Lebanon	Syria	No response	Palestine	Algeria	Egypt
No response	2	3	1	1			
Muslim	10	11	1		2	1	1
Christian	38	2	4	1			

Figure 6: Parents' Birth Place and Religion

diversity facilitator. Reasons for this disparity would be conjectural, except to observe that 80 per cent of the parents involved in the *Diversity Project* came from the coeducational school, where there was a higher number of Christian Iraqis, and only 20 per cent from the girls' school, where the dominant religion among the student cohort was Islam. It is, therefore, reasonable that, as many of the girls' school students came from suburbs often some distance away, parents might find it difficult to attend. Added to this is the fact that these families were large, with children often attending schools at different locations. Hence, it is important to consider these distinctive features behind the graph and, more significantly, to resist the temptation to resort to stereotyping of Muslims as rejecting community engagement. A broader study across secondary schools might well yield very different results.

Family size did appear to be a distinctive feature among the families participating at the two schools. As indicated in Figure 7 below, almost three-quarters of the parents surveyed had more than three children. Parents were not asked to specify exactly how many children they have—rather one, two, three or 'more than three'—but most did provide this information anyway, and the majority in the last category reported that they had five children. In some families there were as many as eight or nine children—one family had twelve—and they ranged in age from their early twenties down to toddler and pre-school age. Of the smaller families of one or two children, all but one were Christian. This small snapshot of Arab and Muslim families appears to confirm the belief that large families are, indeed, preferable among Arabic and Islamic cultures. In just over half the families surveyed (54 per cent) their children were born in Iraq before they travelled to Australia; however, eight of these families also had children after leaving Iraq. Indeed, eleven families had their children while on the move, eight having children in two different countries and three having children across three different countries while in transit. This indicates the significant degree to which some Arab and Muslim students have experienced disruption, not only to continuity of family life, but in terms of their education. Many of the parents surveyed overlooked the question about where their children were born, so it was difficult to ascertain exactly how many families experienced this type of disruption. What is clear from these results,

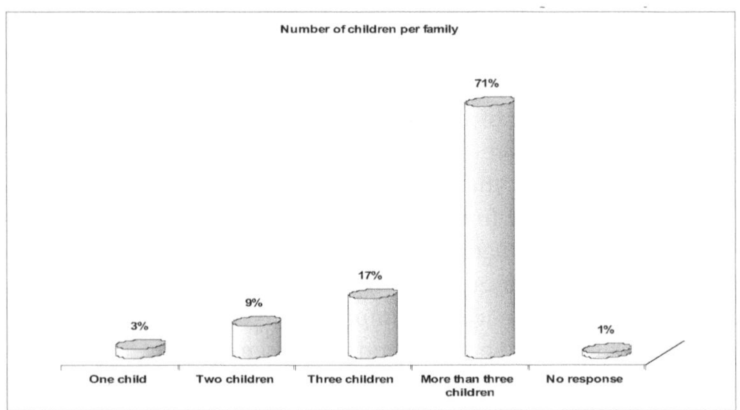

Figure 7: Family

however, is that children in these families enter English-language education in Australia with very little grounding, making their resilience and educational aspirations all the more striking.

Parents with English-language skills were in the minority, numbering 41 per cent of those surveyed. This was spread evenly across women and men. However, it was noted at school meetings that, in most instances, the parents were able to communicate in English to some degree. The 41 per cent indicated in the surveys is probably, therefore, a modest figure and although the surveys distributed were printed in Arabic, it was noted that a small number of parents chose to provide their answers in English. Only one parent, who required assistance completing the survey, was illiterate.

The level of educational experience among the parent cohort revealed higher levels of education among men. Only a third (36 per cent) of the women surveyed had experienced secondary-school education compared to 55 per cent of men. While 49 per cent of women had attended only primary school, and 7 per cent tertiary, 33 per cent of men were educated to primary level, and 9 per cent to tertiary. Education statistics across Australians more generally, however, also find that men in this age group (forties and fifties) are more educated than women. Figures released in 2003 show that around 70 per cent of males in their forties and fifties have at least upper secondary education, compared to between 50 and 60 per cent of females in the same age brackets.[3] It is, therefore, not unusual for women in this age range to be less educated than men. However, the disparity was more marked among this group of Arab and Muslim parents whose secondary education levels were around 20 per cent lower than the average Australian experience. The difference increases considerably when looking at levels of tertiary education, with Australians of this age group generally around three times more likely to have been educated to tertiary level.[4] As earlier studies had found (as discussed in Chapter 2) this does not hamper the educational aspirations among such migrant groups. Indeed, this assertion is supported by this study, which found levels of educational ambition to be very high, often motivated by the desire to fulfil their parents' dreams. However, it does expose a significant level of educational inexperience in some families and this can be exacerbated when parents have poor access to information either through language barriers and/or an ability to attend the school because of shift work, lack of transport or the demands of large families.

The study's surveys and focus-group discussions with parents were a vital element of the *Diversity Project* in helping to develop a more comprehensive understanding of the sorts of issues that face this particular migrant group. While some of the challenges they face are very specific to them, such as the negative perceptions of Arabs and Muslims generated by the media, in other ways their experiences are similar to those encountered by other sections of the CALD community. In particular, the struggle to achieve high educational outcomes can often be attributed to families' lack of familiarity with Australian educational structures and an acquaintance with individual schools' expectations. This can act as a barrier to families' confidence in interacting with teachers and even, in some cases, being present at the school, which some find daunting. The *Diversity Project's* survey of parents sought to understand Arab and Muslim parent engagement with their children's school, not only in terms of *whether* they participate, but whether they *want* to participate. Although 83 per cent of the parents surveyed reported that they 'always' felt comfortable approaching teachers and staff with questions or concerns, there was slightly less confidence when asked how their feedback was considered by the school. Only 57 per cent believed that their feedback was 'definitely' considered seriously by the school. In discussions, some parents reported that they did not want to interfere with their children's education.

In terms of their sense of involvement in the school community, in 2004 not enough parents completed surveys to make the findings meaningful but in 2005 twice as many parents participated. Only 30 per cent said that they were 'very involved' in school life and 39 per cent said that they were 'slightly' involved; however, 61 per cent said that they would like to be 'much more' involved. This was reflected in comments such as: 'I want to attend all meeting [sic] at the school. I want to learn about my kids and their progress in their study and thank you for all your help and for giving our kids a good education.' But in some instances, language posed a frustrating barrier to participation and confidence, as noted by this woman: 'I want to participate in school activities but my problem is the English language.' The 2006 survey was completed by almost twice as many parents again who also expressed a desire for more involvement in the school community. The increase in parent engagement at the schools, and the opportunity to elicit these responses, was made possible by the cultural-diversity facilitator, a role created by the *Diversity Project* in partnership and collaboration with VASS.

Facilitating Arab and Muslim Parent Engagement at School

The presence of the cultural diversity facilitator at the participating schools had been initiated by VASS prior to the commencement of the research phase of the *Diversity Project*. The objective of the community–school partnership facilitated by VASS was to implement a strategy designed around four key areas identified by the transformative model: Policy; Parents; Professional development; and Practice. This strategy is built on the philosophy that improving the educational outcomes for all students requires a holistic approach. By focusing on these four areas, sustainable, structural transformation within schools becomes possible, and the role of a cultural diversity facilitator becomes central to that model. The facilitator's regular meetings with Arab and Muslim parents provided an opportunity for them to clarify the sorts of issues outlined in their own language and among other parents with similar concerns.

This community-building strategy was critical in stimulating a sense of inclusion at the schools. Meetings were convened to provide information in Arabic and Chaldean to help Arab and Muslim parents negotiate school life with more confidence, better understand curriculum expectations and the education system more generally, and help build awareness of support networks available both within the school and in the broader community. It was evident from these community activities at the schools, as well as through the surveys with parents, that many difficulties are encountered by parents when familiarising themselves with an entirely different education system. This is further exacerbated when newly arrived Arab and Muslim parents have had little experience of education themselves, with only primary-level schooling or limited secondary schooling. This can lead them to rely solely on their children to mediate between home and school, putting pressure on the parent–child relationship. For students who have experienced educational discontinuity and even trauma in their country of origin, this can have two main negative impacts upon their families.

First, parents can become confused and alienated from their children's school life, and experience varying degrees of anxiety around whether, and how, they can become involved. Positioning the child as school–home mediator can, therefore, have the reverse effect of actually reducing levels of parent engagement. Some parents were quite aware that their level of involvement in the school community was related to their level of understanding of the school system.

One parent made the linkage between Arab and Muslim parents' misunderstandings of the Australian education system with their level of satisfaction with the school. Through making the correlation between student achievement and parent confidence in understanding the system, he underscored the importance of the cultural diversity facilitator's role in helping familiarise Arab and Muslim families with the Australian educational system. He then extended this idea as an overall social benefit:

> Our experience with the Australian education system is very exciting to us. This education system is totally different than what we used to in all the Arabic countries; therefore, we find difficulties in accepting it without understanding its qualities and properties. The first two years at [the school] we were not satisfied at all but we started to see

some changes that is giving us some hope during this year 2005. In my opinion to improve the relationship between the school, the parents and the children we have to take into consideration the parent concept about the education system here, and we should explain to them the differences between what they used to know (as education system back home) and the education system here that could help in improving the relationship between parents and students in regards to children taking more responsibilities towards their studies. It is very important that the school takes few steps towards encouraging students to take responsibilities in regard to their education (either some sort of punishment and some sort of rewards). There are other point [sic] that I would like to discuss with you in future meetings. I would like to extend to you my appreciation and admiration to this program. In my point of view that program is not restricted to improve the children only but it goes beyond that to help parents progressing and also in the progress of the society.

Once a sense of disconnectedness develops in parents or students, they are at risk of losing touch with their educational goals. Other parents articulated this sense of uncertainty, much of which stems from a lack of confidence in negotiating education in Australia which is unfamiliar and difficult to connect to their previous experience, as articulated by this parent:

My children used to believe that education is very important but when we came to Australia they felt that studying [or education] is not very important and I don't know the reason why: is it the level of education which is not good? Or is it the environment in particular the peer pressure that doesn't encourage the good achievers? That could be the reason why students don't complete their study to get higher education in their future.

This leads us to the second difficulty for families negotiating a foreign education system with little formal education experience of their own. As stated above, only 41 per cent of the parents surveyed claimed knowledge of English, and although this was considered a modest representation, in the majority of instances fluency was limited. It is, therefore, unclear as to whether information contained in school newsletters and notices is filtering through to parents. This communication deficit imposes a need for students to 'educate' their parents about their own education and can add to Arab and Muslim students' pressures to adapt quickly. Some students might simply be unable to cope with these demands without additional support which, in turn, can lead to disengagement. On the other hand, students might use their parents' lack of engagement with school to their short-term advantage. For example, some parents were frustrated that their children never seemed to have any homework and, in fact, were surprised to learn during focus group discussions that the school had high homework expectations and strict homework procedures in place in the form of a diary system to be used between school and home. Some parents were also surprised to learn that there was a homework club run by the school. At Years 9 and 10 levels, which marks the transitional phase into senior secondary school and on to tertiary options, this can have critical consequences. The *Diversity Project* found that there are ways to tackle these obstacles, with a particular focus on Arab and Muslim parents, before they take hold and risk not only their own, but their child's deepening alienation from the education system. The most immediate results came from the *Diversity Project*'s engagement of a multilingual cultural diversity facilitator.

With a view to opening up better communication with parents, the cultural diversity facilitator worked towards establishing an ongoing support network for Arab and Muslim parents. As a core group of parents, it was envisaged that they would become a conduit between school and other parents within their community networks by being fully conversant with the school's requirements and procedures. Working in tandem with the cultural diversity facilitator they would also assist in the translation of information into their community languages, gradually moving the responsibility for communication away from their children. Ultimately, Arab and Muslim parents would represent their community on the school council, which would realise their transition to equal stakeholders within the school community. Progressing towards these goals was formalised by the *Diversity*

Project through a series of modules designed to take Arab and Muslim parents through the issues identified in the research. The first introduces them to the school environment, key staff members, information relating to the purchase of books and uniforms, the operation of the canteen and library, homework expectations and so on. Next, the parents are shown the various educational pathways available to students in the Victorian education system, which can be quite complex. This is designed to reassure all CALD parents and students that there are several opportunities available to students beyond the traditional trajectory of secondary school to university. Third, the parents are given an overview of the Australian educational system, including its curricular framework and rationale, and expectations of students, together with comparative information as to how this might differ from the parents' own experiences overseas. This module is designed to open up discussion with parents in order to broaden their understanding of education in Australia and to alleviate their concerns that their children's experience of school might differ in some ways from their own. Discussion is not, however, limited to this final module in the series. Throughout the *Diversity Project* Arab and Muslim parents were very keen to discuss their children's education and to share their insights. The modules are seen as an important way of harnessing this enthusiasm and engagement.

Measuring the Work of the Cultural Diversity Facilitator

The cultural diversity facilitator established a vital link between parents, teachers and students which showed evidence of closing gaps in Arab and Muslim parents' understanding of the Australian school system; encouraging and facilitating parent–teacher interaction; and opening up a shared understanding of school between teachers, parents and students. The work of the cultural diversity facilitator was designed to provide parents with a wider scope of knowledge about secondary education in Australia and to facilitate their access to school decision-makers. This was a response to their expressed desire to play a more proactive role in their children's education and in the school's organisational structures and social life. But the benefits also extended to their relationships with their children. In 2003, only 20 per cent of Arab and Muslim students surveyed said that they talk to their parents about school and study 'regularly'. In 2005, this had moved up to 54 per cent, a significant improvement and an indication that strengthening parent engagement was working. A particular concern for parents, and for some students, was that they are sometimes required to engage in activities beyond the parameters of school, such as work experience and school camps. The cultural diversity facilitator has been in a position to mediate between parents and school staff to assist parents and students in understanding the rationale behind these programs, the way that they are structured and how they are supervised. This type of individual case management can include referrals to outside agencies where families are in need of additional support, or raising awareness of alternative educational streams available, such as VCAL (Victorian Certificate of Applied Learning) where students might be struggling with the more academic focus of VCE (Victorian Certificate of Education). A lack of understanding about these options, and the rationale behind course choices in the years leading up to VCE Years 11 and 12, can highlight the gulf between parents' own education experience (or inexperience) in their countries of origin and that of their children. However, the disjuncture around Arab and Muslim parents' expectations of secular education in Australia can extend beyond these functional factors and into cultural and religious concerns, as some parents hold 'the essential belief that education is a religious obligation, not a secular process'.[5] Though the *Diversity Project*'s surveys and discussions among Arab and Muslim parents did not affirm this, a level of family anxiety emerged in discussions with students, such as the comment from one girl quoted earlier whose mother believed that school was corrupting her.

Teacher Resources and Curricular Support

The next level of intervention related to teacher training and curriculum resources, referred to as Teacher Support Materials (TSM). This part of the *Diversity Project* was concerned with professional development and practice in the classroom. To this end, a number of structured focus group discussions with teachers and staff took place in the participating schools, where a collaborative approach towards the development of this resource was established. Teachers' views on various aspects of multicultural education and cultural diversity were gauged and their input into the basic architecture and content of the

TSM was also sought. Linking this initiative to the key issues arising from active research with the students to wider educational themes as defined in the VELS, the TSM built a relevant and inclusive teaching resource capable of addressing the students' interests and concerns. Done within the existing curriculum framework, the schools benefited from a cutting edge resource that interacts with policy and curriculum standards. This part of the resource, concerning curriculum and pedagogical practice, was therefore developed through a number of structured focus group discussions in the partnership schools.

Members of staff from the participating schools were engaged in relation to their pedagogical choices and attitudes towards cultural diversity. The *Project* has produced extensive empirical evidence that deals with the extent to which teaching methods (pedagogy) and teaching content (curriculum) can be addressed in these schools in order to effect successful multicultural education. Before teachers and staff engaged more fully with these issues, they attended professional development sessions in which they were canvassed about their views of multicultural education, interaction between teachers and students at their schools, and the impact of external issues on Arab and Muslim Australian students. While it is clear from Figure 8 that teachers were aware, to varying degrees, that external political events did have an impact on their schools, overall, teachers believed

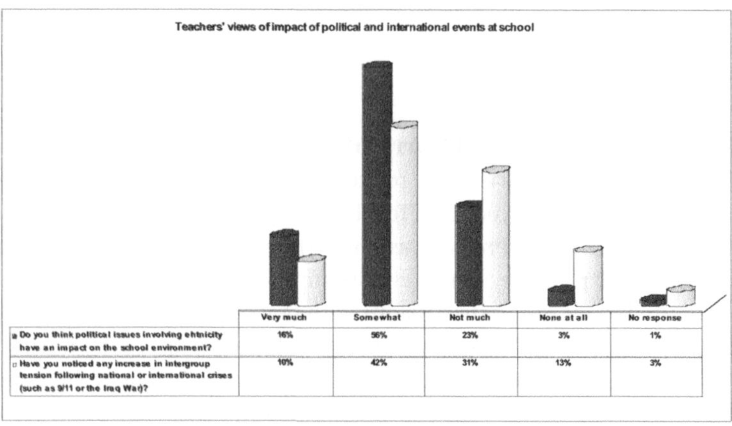

	Very much	Somewhat	Not much	None at all	No response
Do you think political issues involving ehtnicity have an impact on the school environment?	16%	56%	23%	3%	1%
Have you noticed any increase in intergroup tension following national or international crises (such as 9/11 or the Iraq War)?	10%	42%	31%	13%	3%

Figure 8: Teachers' Views of External Events on School

that relationships within the school between ethnic groups were generally sound. Interestingly though, while 83 per cent of teachers thought that there were 'occasional' misunderstandings between teachers and students because of cultural difference, 49 per cent thought that this was the case between students and students.

Teachers were quite clear about the issues where there was the potential for tension to arise, but there was less consensus about exactly what multicultural education was. This was in large part due to demands upon their time which left little available for professional development or for seeking out educational resources beyond the standard curriculum. Online resources were therefore designed to connect teachers to a wide range of multicultural materials and lesson plans that are responsive to the cultural composition of their classrooms, more fully engaging students and teachers in the cultural dynamic within their school community.

The *Project's* TSM initiative provided a central platform through which the key questions and issues arising from students' focus groups and interviews were linked to wider educational policies, such as the VELS and the National Framework for Values Education in Australian Schools. These links respond to the school's existing curriculum framework and to the unique cultural composition of its community. The online resources allow teachers to not only access a range of multicultural materials, but to navigate a variety of cultural vignettes which can then be cross-referenced against policy documents and other relevant links. Before finalising the online TSM, teachers' input was sought again through several interactive professional development sessions to test the resources, a process that will be ongoing as the materials are rolled out to more schools. The core objectives of the *Diversity Project* in general, and the teacher online support resource in particular, were to offer schools and teachers support in dealing with cultural diversity and intercultural relationships. This support is intended and designed to be interactive and reflexive rather than rigid and prescriptive.

The student-based cultural snapshots and related multicultural perspectives provided in the TSM do not form a discrete learning area nor are they meant to be taught in isolation. Instead, they are designed to permeate the school's culture, whether at the level of administrative structures, or teaching resources and practices, or the school's connectedness to its immediate milieu of parents and community organisations. To complement the TSM resources, a collection of lesson plans was designed to help teachers respond in the classroom to culturally specific situations. For example, one of the partnership schools has an English Language Centre that newly arrived CALD students attend before they integrate into mainstream classes and the wider school community. The integration of other CALD students may possibly require a different pedagogical approach to that proposed within the TSM and the lesson plans that it supports. However, the wider cross-cultural conceptual issues tackled in the TSM within the VELS will be of immediate relevance beyond the case studies reported in this book.

The *Diversity Project*'s partnership approach recognises the interdependent nature of the learning experience and the critical role of social and cultural factors in shaping the educational achievements of Arab and Muslim Australians and other CALD students. The findings generated through the research confirm the basic principle of the model, namely that the comparatively lower achievements of Arab and Muslim Australian students were generally reflected in attitudes towards social and cultural environments that are filtered through their parents' understanding of schooling policies and attitudes towards educational achievements. Engaging the community in a more systematic manner has been instrumental, not only in shifting this paradigm, but also in bridging the gap between schools and their immediate communities, particularly where these communities face considerable economic and social obstacles. The *Project's* multidimensional approach has been useful in analysing the many factors that influence educational outcomes for Arab and Muslim students and its ongoing transformative model has been designed to structurally inspire positive change both at the social and educational levels. For this to be achieved an integrated approach has been adopted where schools, parents and communities formed a strategic partnership aimed at reducing the effects of social barriers and cross-cultural tensions.

Overall, school environment and policy change was the *Diversity Project's* long term goal. To achieve this, change has been sought on a policy level. One participating school, in consultation with the research team, for example, has already enshrined a 'Cultural Diversity Charter' and a similar charter is envisaged in cooperation with other schools. This initiative responds directly to the *Multicultural Victoria Act 2004*, which enshrines principles of access, participation and contribution, for all Victorian citizens, to services made available by the Victorian Government. Schools are encouraged to be aware of the Act and Victoria's Department of Education and Early Childhood Development website advises how it applies to school councils, principals, school staff and students.

Recent policy directives on the management of cultural diversity in schools are consistent with a new approach that seems to recognise the more fluid demographic reality of educational institutions, but fails to enact such policies through appropriate resource allocation and teacher training. In fact, one can argue that this state of affairs is a by-product of neo-liberal thinking, as it stipulates that schools meet new standards and be more accountable while at the same time face reduced funding. It is within such a political context that the schools participating in the study reported in this book have been operating over the last few years: Increased student numbers as some schools close down; increased linguistic and cultural diversity among student populations; static or shrinking resources; and ever-increasing emphasis on measurable outcomes and learning standards. For students of Arab and Muslim background the challenges within this educational setting are further compounded by the wider social discursive representations of their culture and religion as being closely associated with sources of insecurity, both socially within Australia and on the political and military front internationally.

Notes

1 See, for example, research by S Rothman and J McMillan, 2003, *Longitudinal Surveys of Australian Youth Research Report 36: Influences on Achievement in Literacy and Numeracy*, Australian Council for Educational Research, Melbourne.
2 Progress of the review of the Federal Government's Living in Harmony and Harmony Day programs can be found at www.harmony.gov.au.

3   Gene Tunny, *Educational Attainment in Australia*, Australian Treasury.
       See www.treasury.gov.au/documents/1107/PDF/01Educationl.pdf,
       viewed 8 July 2008.
4   ibid.
5   Abdullah Saeed and Shahram Akbarzadeh, 2001, *Muslim Communities
       in Australia*, UNSW Press, Sydney, p. 121.

Chapter 5

Education, Multiculturalism and the Wider Social Challenge

Pierre Bourdieu famously argued that there was a need 'to reconcile the demands of education for society and the economy with the personal needs of individual development'.[1] Indeed, what this book has tried to argue is that, in addition to centralised policies, local solutions are possible and, in fact, essential to meet the needs of individual students, in particular those from lower socio-economic backgrounds and other marginalised groups. In the case of students from Arab and Muslim backgrounds, these localised solutions became even more necessary in the aftermath of the 'war on terror'.

The terrorist attacks on New York and the Pentagon in 2001 marked a critical shift towards an 'us and them' discourse, characterised so contentiously by Samuel P Huntington as a 'clash of civilizations', that has cemented what is perceived as an insuperable difference dividing two monolithic, monotheistic traditions. When George W Bush referred to America's retaliation against terrorists as a 'crusade' he seemed unaware of his historically insensitive transgression. Bush, however, went on to exploit a sense of irretrievable bipolarity with his subsequent statement 'you are either with us or against us in the fight against terror[2]' as a coalition of Western states began its invasion of Afghanistan. On a local level, this rhetoric of fundamental difference and fear reached fertile soil in Australia and an internal struggle to restrain the Muslim 'other' has become increasingly confrontational.

The Muslim as 'other' had already taken hold of the Australian imagination with the media's characterisation of Lebanese youth gangs in Sydney since the late 1990s. These 'gangs', engaged in 'territorial battles' with Vietnamese gangs, are portrayed as operating outside the legal, civil and institutional framework underpinned by 'our' British-Christian core. It was the centrality of this inheritance that formed the foundations of the White Australia Policy, but even thirty years after its formal dismantling, just beneath Australia's idealised multicultural surface has lingered a mistrust of difference that at times appears difficult to shift. Indeed, 'contemporary anxieties about race and immigration confirm the residual influence of White Australia[3]', and this disquiet about the retention of Australia's Anglo-Celtic heritage was often substantiated by former prime minister John Howard in his invocations of 'our' British inheritance. With the aid of the media, events such as the rape conviction and severe sentencing of Lebanese youths in Sydney in 2000, the arrest of Muslim terror suspects in Melbourne and Sydney, and the Cronulla riots in 2005 have exacerbated public suspicions about the capricious criminal nature of, in particular, young Middle Eastern men. This sort of panic about the unpredictable 'other' replaces an earlier Australian fixation with the 'yellow peril' or 'Asian invasion' undermining Australia's Anglo-Celtic stability. The domestication of 'terror' and the appearance of a military etymology used to articulate urban fears of 'invasion' and 'attack', therefore, pre-date the 'war on terror' and recall earlier national anxieties.

If the September 11 attacks lead some to portray Muslims and Arabs as capable of committing atrocious acts, then the invasion of Iraq has raised doubts about the loyalty and attachment of Arab and Muslim Australians who were portrayed in some circles as sympathetic to 'the enemy'. When the United States, Britain and Australia declared war on Iraq on 20 March 2003, many members of the Arab and Muslim communities knew that they were likely to face increased vilification and harassment. These apprehensions were rooted in similar experiences during the 1990–91 Gulf War, when Muslim and Arab communities in Australia were subjected to considerable hostility and xenophobia. Indeed, as public consultations[4] and research have shown, 'people reported being fired from their jobs or refused employment or promotion because of their race or religion. Children have been bullied in school yards. Women have been stalked, abused and assaulted in shopping centres ... "Terrorist", "Dirty Arab", "Murderer", "Bloody Muslim", "Raghead", "bin Laden", "Illegal Immigrant" and "Black C ... t" are just some of the labels and profanities[5]' that were used against members of the Arab and Muslim communities. Many among Arab and Muslim Australians have had their sense of belonging to Australian society undermined and, in some cases, their loyalties questioned. The following statement to Parliament by the then–prime minister was ironically meant to offer support for Arab and Muslim Australians and allay their fears in an increasingly suspicious society:

> Australia is home to several hundred thousand people of Middle Eastern background. We welcomed them ... and we appreciate their contribution to our nation. Many of them could be torn between seeing Saddam brought to account and the possible dangers facing their families back in Iraq. During this time, they will need our compassion and our support.[6]

In this statement, while offering words of sympathy and solidarity with Australians of Middle Eastern background, and particularly Iraqi-Australians, the former prime minister still retains and reinforces the centrality of the dominance of the Anglo-Celtic core of Australia. He states that 'we' welcomed 'them', that their becoming part of Australia was conditional upon wider Australian support, and that 'they' have contributed to 'our nation'. Howard's appraisal then seems to suggest that Australians of Middle Eastern background cannot claim the same ownership of and belonging to the Australian nation that his statement implies Anglo-Australians can. His intimation at divided nationalist loyalties to another nation appears to explain why he thinks this is so—that there is not the full loyalty to Australia among migrants that white Australians inherently exhibit.

When students were asked whether they thought that Arab and Muslim Australians were positively perceived in Australian society, the majority at the coeducational school (72 per cent) answered 'somewhat'. This suggested some caution, with only 13 per cent of the coeducational students reporting 'clearly positive', but only 6 per cent choosing 'negative'. Students from the girls' school were more overtly positive. Thirty-seven per cent believed that Australians perceive Arab-Australians well and 47 per cent thought that this was 'somewhat' the case. But over twice as many girls'-school students (17 per cent) opted for a negative response—14 per cent 'not much' and 3 per cent 'not at all'. Some girls in each of the groups surveyed at both schools wore the hijab, although a higher proportion was found at the girls' school. Nevertheless, all girls were aware of the sometimes negative experiences of Muslim women in their communities. A female student from Year 10 attending the coeducational school, for example, observed: 'I think Australia is a good country but sometimes Muslim ladies get treated very badly and differently. I think it should be a country of real freedom. And ladies with the hijab should feel free to do whatever they wish.'

This again confirms that the community is a less certain, even a sometimes threatening, place for some Arab and Muslim Australian students. When students of non-Arabic-speaking background were asked the same question the following year (in 2006), 71 per cent of them also believed that Arab-Australians were only 'somewhat' positively perceived by the Australian community. However, a greater

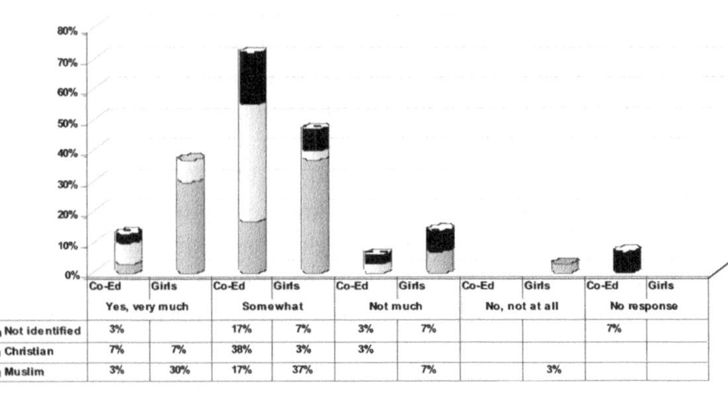

	Yes, very much		Somewhat		Not much		No, not at all		No response	
	Co-Ed	Girls	Co-Ed	Girls	Co-Ed	Girls	Co-Ed	Girls	Co-Ed	Girls
Not identified	3%		17%	7%	3%	7%			7%	
Christian	7%	7%	38%	3%	3%					
Muslim	3%	30%	17%	37%		7%		3%		

Figure 9: Perceptions of Arab-Australians

number of the non-Arab-Muslim group (19 per cent) opted for the negative responses, 17 per cent answering 'not much' and 2 per cent 'not at all'.

Among coeducational students, a stronger response was recorded when asked whether they believed that they themselves were positively perceived by Australian society. Despite students' awareness of some social hostility towards Arab-Australians, they had sufficient self-awareness to realise that the actions of some, who are completely disconnected from their world, ought not to affect them personally. Forty-one per cent of coeducational students answered 'yes, very much' when asked if they, personally, were positively perceived compared to only 13 per cent in the previous question. The girls'-school cohort answering 'yes, very much' increased over time by only 4 per cent, and 6 per cent more answered 'somewhat'. But again, girls were a little more negative about perceptions of their, and their communities', identity than the coeducational students with 14 per cent opting for a negative response compared to only 6 per cent of coeducational students. Overall, however, there was a hint of greater confidence around self-perception, possibly because students believe that the wider society would have no reason to develop negative perceptions about them personally. A Year 10 student from the girls' school was aware that perceptions can often be generated out of ignorance in the community: 'Some people look at other people and

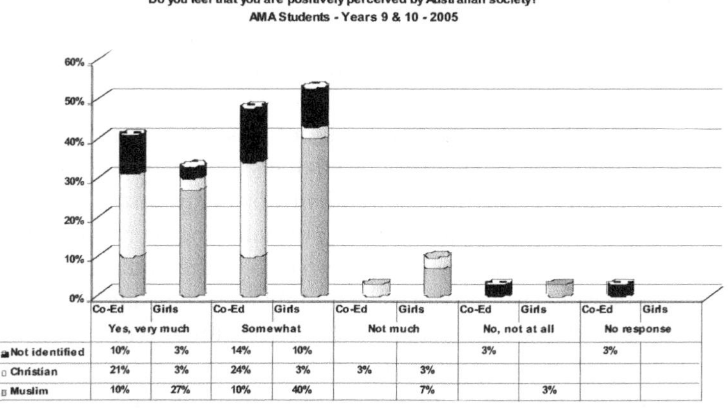

	Yes, very much		Somewhat		Not much		No, not at all		No response	
	Co-Ed	Girls	Co-Ed	Girls	Co-Ed	Girls	Co-Ed	Girls	Co-Ed	Girls
Not identified	10%	3%	14%	10%			3%		3%	
Christian	21%	3%	24%	3%	3%	3%				
Muslim	10%	27%	10%	40%		7%		3%		

Figure 10: Students' Perceptions of Themselves

judge them without even knowing who they are or where they come from. Most of the time people judge them badly.'

While students were at least somewhat positive about perceptions of themselves and Arab and Muslim Australians in the community more generally, as indicated in Figures 8 and 9, the issue of racism elicited more divided views. Just over half the coeducational students (52 per cent) believed 'very much' that racism is a big problem in Australia. This compared with one-third (33 per cent) of girls'-school students. When combining the responses 'yes, very much' and 'somewhat' to understand what percentage of students believe that racism is a problem in Australia, the result is almost identical: 73 per cent at the coeducational and 72 per cent at the girls' school. This is quite a high proportion; three-quarters of the students in the Arab and Muslim community surveyed believe that they live in a racist country.

The recent conflicts in the Middle East have clearly impacted on both Arab and Muslim Australians. The forms these impacts take and how they may be measured vary. One recent study shows that the racism and xenophobia expressed towards Arab and Muslim Australians by other Australians is currently at alarmingly high levels.[7] A study that surveyed over 5000 residents in Queensland and New South Wales in December 2001 found that anti-Muslim and anti–Middle Eastern sentiment was very strong, with both communities mentioned most commonly as groups that respondents believed did not fit into Australian society.[8] Moreover, non-Muslim women were more concerned about marriage of a non-Muslim woman to a Muslim man than vice versa, suggesting that 'Muslims suffer quite dramatically from the stereotypes of Islamic misogyny/sexism'.[9] Not only did the findings show that high degrees of hostility are felt towards Muslim Australians, but it also showed that spontaneous, non-formal types of racism are experienced frequently by many Australians, such as disrespectful treatment, mistrust and labelling or name-calling. This is what is now increasingly referred to in the literature as new forms of racism.[10] The survey suggested that a significant proportion of Arab and Muslim Australians experienced these types of racism through everyday social interaction.[11]

Similarly, the same percentage of students in each school (20 per cent) thought that racism was 'not much' of a problem, and only

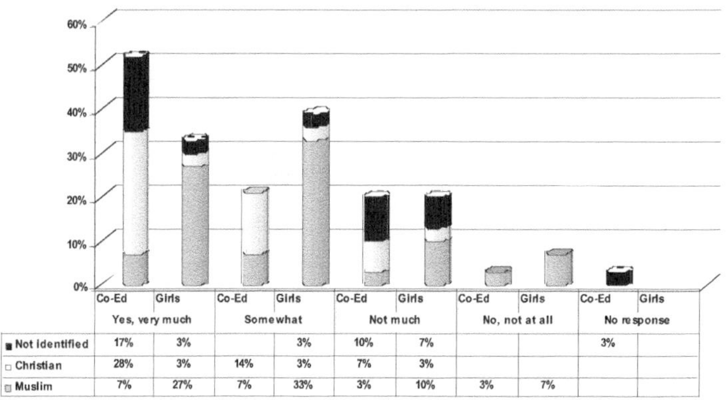

	Co-Ed	Girls	Co-Ed	Girls	Co-Ed	Girls	Co-Ed	Girls	Co-Ed	Girls
	Yes, very much		Somewhat		Not much		No, not at all		No response	
Not identified	17%	3%		3%	10%	7%			3%	
Christian	28%	3%	14%	3%	7%	3%				
Muslim	7%	27%	7%	33%	3%	10%	3%	7%		

Figure 11: Racism in Australia

small numbers of students thought it was not a problem at all. Some students, although a minority, were sensitive to racism in terms of their own identity, as reflected in the comment of one Muslim boy from Year 10, who added: 'No comments because you will get offended. But I have a lot of issues about racism and this survey.'

When non-Arab and non-Muslim students were asked this same question more recently, in 2006, an identical number of students (73 per cent) believed that racism is a problem in Australia: 46 per cent 'very much' and 27 per cent 'somewhat'. This group of students was drawn from a wide range of cultural backgrounds, including English, Vietnamese, Spanish, Indian and Finnish. Racism, even among significantly diverse groups, is recognised as present in Australian society. A Vietnamese boy from Year 10 observed: 'I think racism is a very big problem. Racism is irrelevant and there is also no point. Everyone should get along with each other and no-one should put each other down because they are different. Australia is a multicultural country and everyone must respect each other.'

Though the study focused on the experiences of racism among students in schools, it was revealing that all students surveyed were also very much attuned to wider societal discourses on and actual practices of racism outside of the school arenas. This is not surprising given that schools are a microcosm of society at large and as such do

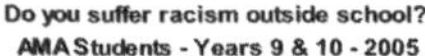

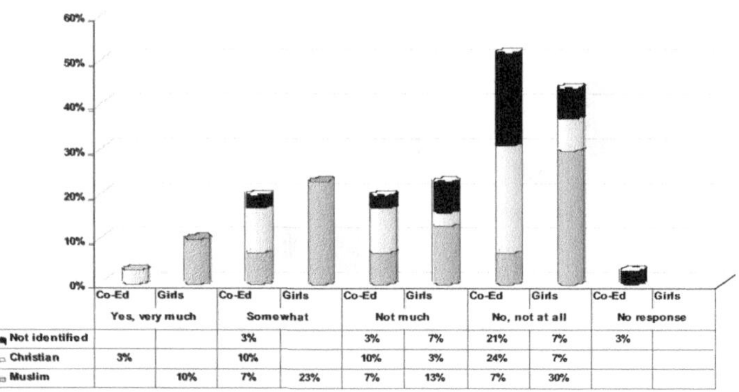

| | Yes, very much | | Somewhat | | Not much | | No, not at all | | No response | |
	Co-Ed	Girls	Co-Ed	Girls	Co-Ed	Girls	Co-Ed	Girls	Co-Ed	Girls
Not identified			3%		3%	7%	21%	7%	3%	
Christian	3%		10%		10%	3%	24%	7%		
Muslim		10%	7%	23%	7%	13%	7%	30%		

Figure 12: Personal Experience of Racism

reflect to a large degree the same social and economic dynamics affecting the wider societal environment within which they operate. The above graph illustrates students' experiences of racism outside of the school boundaries:

Although some girls in particular had experienced or witnessed hostility due to their cultural or religious background, almost half of those surveyed (48 per cent) indicated they have had personal experiences of racism. Fifty-two per cent of the coeducational students had not experienced racism at all outside school, compared to 44 per cent from the girls' school. Almost identical numbers of students at each school—20 per cent and 23 per cent respectively—answered 'not much' and 'somewhat', while 10 per cent of girls from the girls' school, all of whom were Muslim, said that they suffer racism 'very much' compared to only 3 per cent from the coeducational school. The survey revealed that Muslim girls do appear to be more aware of, and sensitive to, racism and even though this manifested on a small scale in this survey, racism in Australia is clearly an issue that students from a range of backgrounds are aware is present. A Year 10 student from the girls' school understood the dimensions of racism when she added: 'It isn't just racism of background, it is racism of culture and religion that also affects people in the community.'

Students were very much aware of wider community debates and media attention directed towards their cultural and religious groups, which made them feel ill at ease and powerless in their ability to respond. These tensions are felt quite distinctly by girls as opposed to boys for a range of reasons, not least because of the gender-specific images of male and female Muslims projected in the media. Added to this is the prevailing sense of moral ambiguity in Australia that creates anxiety for some young members of the Muslim community. For girls in particular, the uncertainty of precisely what private moral values to adhere to in Australian society poses a range of difficulties at secondary school, for example, where issues such as sexuality, sexual health, teenage pregnancy and drug use form a part of the curriculum. These issues are morally challenging for Muslims (and many other groups as well), causing concern among parents who already often feel alienated from the school system, and additional pressures for young people learning to reconcile public and private life. Muslim girls growing up in Australia can be particularly burdened by external social and internal family pressures around morality. While they know that 'Islam requires that both men and women be chaste and seek successful relationships in marriage', and that the virginity of *both* sexes is expected[12], girls are also aware of double standards around male sexuality before marriage, increasing the burden of their moral responsibility. In focus group discussions, some Year 9 students expressed shock about what they observed in their neighbourhoods. (Further detail on these anxieties can be found in Chapter 3.)

The media's essentialised representation of Muslim males and females can add to this moral confusion and exacerbate the pressures of assimilation for young girls who feel that they cannot possibly emulate this sort of behaviour. Another difficulty for young women is the issue of wearing the hijab, which contributes to characterisations in the West of Muslim women as repressed and, as was evident at the 2003 anti-war protest discussed in Chapter 1, makes them easily identifiable. Many Muslim women, however, describe a sense of empowerment when wearing the scarf, as for them it equalises gender subjectivity. For Muslim women, therefore, a binary emerges whereby they are represented in the popular, secular media as oppressed but within their own communities feel empowered by Islam.[13]

Several studies have been undertaken that confirm the media's inflammation of gender stereotypes. For example, a report commissioned by the Human Rights and Equal Opportunity Commission

(HREOC) into the experience of racism among Muslim and Arab Australians since 11 September 2001, cites several examples of Muslims, mostly women, being terrorised in their neighbourhoods: 'Jamila explained how her being insulted and menaced on a Melbourne train by two men was directly related to a commercial current affairs program the night before about gang rapes in Sydney and the purported endemic violence and misogyny of Muslim youth.'[14]

It seems particularly ironic that non-Muslim men would behave aggressively towards women in response to their belief that young male Muslims engage in acts of 'violence and misogyny'.

Girls from the all girls' school participating in this study were nevertheless very positive about life in Australia and held aspirations that did not differentiate them from any other cultural group:

> I think that I'm really lucky to be living in Australia because it's a country of freedom. And everyone here is equalised with the human rights. I'm looking forward to finishing my education here in the incoming future.

> I think Australia is the perfect place for me to live in because I'm a peaceful person that is free and hates war!! I'm looking forward to Year 12 and completing my exams and getting my average so I can finish uni and achieve something in my life!!

The student surveys reflected a generally positive response to school, and optimism about future learning. What seemed most evident from the surveys was the sense of security that Arab and Muslim Australian students derive from school. In both of the participating schools there was a high percentage of students born overseas, particularly in the Middle East, and students from similar language groups. This would most likely have added to their strong sense of belonging within their school communities, generating a bonding through experiences of re-settlement, but more broadly a sense of shared experience with students from diverse backgrounds. Areas that reflected some uneasiness revolved around issues of racism and perceptions of the Arab and Muslim community. Girls of Muslim background were clearly more likely to express some doubt about the way they, and Muslim women generally, are perceived. Several of these girls, or women in their families, wore the hijab and this sense of being conspicuous as 'different' seemed to contribute to their close bonds with other Muslim girls at school. Boys appeared less likely to express any social awkwardness about their identity; however, on an academic level they exhibited slightly less confidence than girls. Encouragement from parents and family to do well at school and to pursue tertiary studies was evident among each survey group at participating schools, with no gender distinctions drawn in terms of future aspirations.

More specific accounts of attacks and vilification of Arab and Muslim Australians, particularly women, can be widely located, though these tend to be secondhand accounts. For example, a community cultural development worker relates some of the incidents that she has encountered through her community work and when working on a hotline set up to take calls about racial attacks at the time of the US-led invasion of Iraq:

> [T]here was a story about a Muslim woman, who was wearing hijab, having coffee when a group of boys got out of a car and dragged her across the road by her scarf. She sustained serious back injuries as a result. There's stories about the many girls who have been threatened by rape. Schools have had threats of rape. Death threats.[15]

Other reports of Arab and Muslim Australians' experiences seem to verify such accounts of verbal and physical assault; women being threatened with rape; scarves being ripped off; being spat on, intimidated and patronised; receiving hate mail; obscene phone calls and death threats; the firebombing of mosques and bomb threats; stoning of a Muslim school's bus carrying children; and the inciting of hate in the media, particularly on talkback radio.[16] Muslim women in particular appear to be targeted for two major reasons. First, those who wear hijab, or a headscarf, tend to be individuals who are most physically and visibly identifiable with Islam.[17] Second, as research substantiates[18], Muslim women are viewed by some Australians as subservient, complicit in their own oppression by a patriarchal religious and cultural order, and consequently despised.

Racialised Discourse and the New Threatening 'Other'

Perhaps the most disturbing aspect of the media coverage of these issues is that many commentators seamlessly fuse together recent world events, such as September 11 and the Iraq war, with outbursts of discrimination and racism against Arab and Muslim Australians. The correlation seems, to some, to be obvious; however, it is worth exploring more deeply how these members of the Australian community have come to be implicated in events that, in reality, are far beyond their control. This might be understood through the conflation of Muslim and Arab, the lack of understanding of Islam in Western cultures, and the presentation of Islam as a homogeneous entity that is now associated with terrorists' targeting of Westerners. It might also be regarded as part of a conservative backlash against multiculturalism, or at least a conservative hardening of the notion of multiculturalism, reviving fear and deep suspicion of any Australian with multiple cultural and national allegiances, particularly those who are visibly different (and do not assimilate with Anglo norms).

Xenophobic rhetoric towards Arab and Muslim Australians, however, cannot be solely viewed in the context of recent world events, as these communities in Australia have had a long history of exclusion and prejudicial treatment that is also reflective of a broader problematic Western discourse on Islam.

The Historical Homogeneity of Discourse on Islam

There is little doubt that historically Arab and Muslim Australians have been collectively subjected to harassment, prejudice and exclusion from the wider society. Recent violence and abuse, however, appears to have exceeded the intensity of experience around the time of the 1991 Gulf War.[19] Historically, Arab and Muslim Australians have faced discrimination and have been subjected to negative, xenophobic characterisations by Australians. How, then, are we to understand this domestic response to Arab and Muslim Australians within a broader framework that *pre-dates* September 11, 2001?

The public and political discourse emanating from certain Western countries in relation to regional conflicts has led to a problematic association of Islam with 'extremism, intolerance and violence'.[20] Such events include the Iranian revolution of 1979, the

Arab-Israeli conflict, the Gulf War of 1990–91, and terrorist activities undertaken around the world committed in the name of Islam, for example in the Middle East, the Philippines and Indonesia.[21] Therefore, such a causal relationship between the creeds of Islam and Arabs on the one hand, and political violence and oppression on the other, has not been constructed solely as a result of the events of 11 September 2001.

> Anti-Arab racism in the West has a long genealogy. One of the most important aspects of its formation is that it is intricately related to the genealogy of anti-Muslim sentiments. In both the academic orientalist tradition analysed by Edward Said, and the dominant popular Western racist imaginary the boundaries between being an Arab and being a Muslim is greatly blurred.[22]

Certainly such a negative and essentialist discourse has been heightened in the aftermath of the recent terrorists attacks, though it must be emphasised that it is by no means a new addition to the continuum of Western discourse on Islam and the Arabs. In fact, 'malicious generalizations about Islam have become the last acceptable form of denigration of foreign culture in the West'.[23] The 'clash of civilizations' thesis epitomised by Samuel P Huntington, where Islam is portrayed as a 'single, coherent entity' that is forever and inevitably on a path towards violent conflict with 'the West' is portrayed as fixed:[24]

> So long as Islam remains Islam (which it will) and the West remains the West (which is more dubious), this fundamental conflict between two great civilizations and ways of life will continue to define their relations to the future even as it has defined them for the past fourteen centuries.[25]

Such sweeping and hostile generalisations deny Islam its diversity in terms of character, practices and beliefs, and present Muslims and Arabs as having intrinsic natures that are mostly discussed pejoratively.[26] This has dangerous consequences for inciting hatred and distrust towards Muslims and those in the West associated with Islam:

The deliberately created associations between Islam and fundamentalism ensure that the average reader comes to see Islam and fundamentalism as essentially the same thing. Given the tendency to reduce Islam to a handful of rules, stereotypes, and generalizations about the faith, its founder, and all of its people, then the reinforcement of every negative fact associated with Islam—its violence, primitiveness, atavism, threatening qualities—is perpetuated.[27]

This shows that well before September 11, the Western imagination constructed an Islamic totality that is associated with violence, oppression and terror. The social and psychological impacts of recent events on Arab and Muslim Australians, therefore, must be understood as being a product of a long history of antagonism and misunderstanding towards Islam and Arabs by many sections of Western society.

While world events involving Muslims, both recent and historical, and their analyses in Western media and other forums have shaped much of the anti-Arab and anti-Muslim sentiment felt in Australia, such sentiment cannot be understood solely in these terms. Australia as a nation has a long history of formal and informal exclusion of racialised 'others', those Australians who are not part of the dominant Anglo cultural elite, which is shaped by Judeo-Christian values. While there are historical specificities that result in particular ethnic and religious groups being marginalised for different reasons at particular points in time, what is evident in the case of Arab and Muslim Australians is that there are commonalities in Australia's exclusion of minority groups that exist across the experiences of various ethnic and cultural groups.

Multiculturalism in Australia: What Future for Muslims?
Whilst current debates about the advantages and disadvantages of multiculturalism would seem to be a direct product of the current economic and security concerns, the questioning of the capacity of Muslim migrants to integrate into Australia and other Western societies is not a totally new phenomenon. A well documented historical trend has been established since World War I, whereby Anglo-Celtic Australians have doubted Arab and Muslim Australians' allegiances to

the Australian nation in times of world crises involving Muslims or Arabs.[28] While some Muslim-Australians have reacted by prompting their community to self-consciously promote a positive image of Islam in Australia and win the trust of non-Muslim Australians, other Muslims feel that this is 'burdening the victim' and appeases those who perpetuate hatred towards them.[29] Such hostility and questioning of Muslim-Australians has naturally caused fear, apprehension and isolation among some in their communities and effectively silenced them:

> There had always been a certain social distance between non-Muslims and orthodox Muslims … but now Muslims faced an abyss and overnight they had become non-people. The reaction was far worse than it had been ten years before during the Gulf War … [O]ther Muslims retreated and became silent because they did not believe they would receive a 'fair go'.[30]

Arab and Muslim Australians have often been reduced to the same monolith of pejorative stereotypical images of Islam identified by Said. This reductionism denies them their cultural diversity and, whatever the rhetoric around cultural pluralism, the Anglo-Celtic influence remains the most dominant and critically undermines their identity:

> What is constantly ignored by 'Muslim watchers' in Australia is the enormous diversity among Australian Muslims, for everyone is not cut from the one cloth: differences in education, socioeconomic background, ethnicity, customs and religious outlook play their part … Stereotypes now define people as less than human and what a litany there is to choose from: veiled women, fierce bearded men, barbaric parents, rapists and suicide bombers—these are the images taken to represent Islam.[31]

To make sense of the current negative images and representations of Arab and Muslim Australians, it is important to look for, and acknowledge, historical parallels as a way of unlocking the present anomalies. Like anti-Semitism, Islamophobia in Western societies has been fuelled by a history of religious competition and antagonism. As Said has pointed out, orientalism, or the Western construction of a negative image of the Orient, carries within it the stamp of a problematic attitude towards Islam:

> Islam was a real provocation in many ways. It lay uneasily close to Christianity, it could boast of unrivalled military and political successes. Nor was this all ... From the end of the seventh century until the battle of Lepanto in 1571, Islam in either its Arab, Ottoman, or North African and Spanish form dominated or effectively threatened European Christianity. That Islam outstripped and outshone Rome cannot have been absent from the mind of any European past or present.[32]

While these stereotypes originate in Europe and more recently America, they are increasingly propagated in environments such as Australia, even so far as making their way into school textbooks[33], through the media and Hollywood.[34] The report of the National Inquiry into Racist Violence in Australia noted that anti-Arab and anti-Muslim feelings are largely stereotyped by violence, terrorism and hostage-taking, and that religious fundamentalism, conservative attitudes towards women and morality, and conspicuous dress are 'un-Australian' values.

Global events are, in reality, far beyond the control of Arab and Muslim Australians. Misleading perceptions, however, might be understood through a tendency of some in the West to conflate Muslim and Arab identity and to represent Islam as a homogeneous entity associated with terrorism targeted at Westerners. Negative perceptions of Muslims and Arabs also need to be located within a broader conservative backlash against multiculturalism that is manifesting in increased fear and suspicion of migrants. In other words, the conservative social agenda is increasingly intolerant of visibly different communities who are perceived as not desiring assimilation, and whose perceived multiple allegiances (as outlined earlier) are seen as indicators of 'disloyalty' to the Australian nation-state. Ironically, the social isolation that has been effectively forced upon some members of Muslim and Arab communities has been misinterpreted as a rejection of, and dissociation from, 'Australianness', and as evidence of a deeper loyalty to a religious or political ideology that is presented as the new 'enemy' of the West.

True, the level of racial discrimination and vilification experiences suffered by many Arab and Muslim Australians at present appears to have exceeded the intensity of negative experiences around the time of the first Gulf War.[35] Yet, it is also true that Arab and Muslim Australians have faced serious levels of discrimination throughout the history of their settlement in Australia[36], and many relate stories of continued harassment and xenophobia throughout the turbulent 1990s. How we understand xenophobia before September 11 is, therefore, crucial to how we understand its insidious reappearance.

The approach adopted by the *Diversity Project* has been useful in analysing this range of social factors influencing educational outcomes for Arab and Muslim Australian students. In addition, it has developed a 'transformative' model to counter the negative tendencies exhibited since September 11 and effect positive change in the school environment, both at the social and the educational levels. To this end, an integrated approach engaging parents and communities in a strategic partnership aimed at reducing the effects of social barriers, intercultural tension and racism has worked alongside the active research among students that has been discussed here.

Notes

1   Michael Grenfell, 2004, *Pierre Bourdieu, Agent Provocateur*, Continuum, London and New York, p. 56.
2   *CNN.com*, 2001, 'You are Either With Us or Against Us in the Fight Against Terror', 6 November, http://archives.cnn.com/2001/US/11/06/gen.attack.on.terror/.
3   Gwenda Tavan, 2005, *The Long, Slow Death of White Australia*, Scribe Publications, Melbourne, p. 239.
4   HREOC, *Isma*.
5   ibid., p. iii.
6   John Howard, quoted in M Kingston 2003, 'Howard's Case: The Missing Links', *Sydney Morning Herald*, 5 February.
7   See KM Dunn, 2003, 'Racism in Australia: Findings of a Survey on Racist Attitudes and Experiences of Racism', National Europe Centre Paper no. 77 presented at the conference 'The Challenges of Immigration and Integration in the European Union and Australia', University of Sydney, Sydney, 18–20 February.

8   ibid., p. 2–4.
9   ibid., p. 4.
10   ibid.
11   ibid., p. 10.
12   Jamal and Chandab, p. 58.
13   Sharam Akbarzadeh and Bianca Smith, 2005, *The Representation of Islam and Muslims in the Media*, Monash University sponsored by The Myer Foundation: pp. 30–1.
14   Scott Poynting and Greg Noble, 2004, *Living with Racism: The Experience and Reporting by Arab and Muslim Australians of Discrimination, Abuse and Violence since 11 September 2001*, report to The Human Rights and Equal Opportunity Commission, 19 April, p. 12.
15   Lena Nahlous, 2001, 'Women, Violence and the Media', paper presented at the conference 'Women Reporting Violence in a Time of War', Sydney University of Technology, 8 November, http://international.activism.hss.uts.edu.au/conferences/w_violence/transcripts/nahlous.html, viewed 18 June 2007.; see also ibid.
16   See, for example, Saeed, *Islam in Australia*, pp. 182, 189–92.
17   For this linkage between the physical identifiers of some Muslim women and attacks upon Muslim women, see also ibid., p. 182.
18   See, for example, Dunn, 'Racism in Australia', p. 4.
19   Saeed, *Islam in Australia*, p. 182.
20   ibid., p. 184.
21   ibid., pp. 184–6.
22   Ray Jureidini and Ghassan Hage, 2002, 'The Australian Arabic Council: Anti-Racist Activism', in Ghassan Hage (ed.), *Arab-Australians Today*, pp. 173–91.
23   Edward W Said, 1997, *Covering Islam: How the Media and the Experts Determine How We See the Rest of the World*, Vintage Books, London, p. xii.
24   ibid., in particular see p. xvi.
25   Samuel P Huntington, 2002, *The Clash of Civilizations and the Remaking of the World Order*, Simon & Schuster, London, p. 212.
26   Said, *Covering Islam*, in particular see pp. xi–xxii.
27   ibid., p. xvi.
28   Saeed, *Islam in Australia*, pp.186–7.
29   Deen, p. 271–9.
30   ibid., pp. 280–3.
31   ibid., pp. 283–7.
32   Edward W Said, 1978, *Orientalism: Western Conceptions of the Orient*, Penguin Books, London, p. 74.
33   For example, see research by AW Ata 1984, 'Moslem Arab Portrayal in the Australian Press and in School Textbooks', *Australian Journal of Social Issues*, vol. 19, no. 3, p. 198; and Dunn, 'Racism in Australia'.
34   Hage, *Against Paranoid Nationalism*; see also Jureidini, in Hage, p. 175.
35   See HREOC, *Isma*.
36   Stevens, pp. 139–66.

CHAPTER 6

Conclusion

This discussion of the experience of Muslims and Arabs in Howard's Australia post–September 11 recalls the stereotypical images of Islam that Edward Said described in the 1980s and 1990s. It is not difficult to recognise Said's 'orientalism' being played out in Australia's anti-Arab and anti-Muslim sentiment through Australian migration history, from the nineteenth through to the twenty-first century. However, in the much-hyped 'age of terror' an altogether new phenomenon is taking fears of the 'other' into unfamiliar terrain, where the perceived adversaries of the West are no longer 'out there' but might be sitting next to us as we travel to work on the train.

Since September 2001, this stoking of public anxieties has accelerated, from the social vilification of Muslims that might have seen a primary-school student teased about 'having a bomb in her pencil case' to Australia's first test of its 'terror' legislation which, at the time of writing, was provoking serious political, legal and diplomatic controversy. Contemporary global political events have undoubtedly contributed to a resurgent fortress mentality in Australia and affected profoundly the lived experiences of its young Arab and Muslim populations. How these 'ambient fears [that] dominate the political landscape[1]' influence their conceptualisations of identity, experiences of education, and ability to respond to political pressure to integrate, call for a new discourse that moves beyond the somewhat exhausted, but tenacious, questions of 'orientalism' and 'multiculturalism'.

Whatever perceptions we might promote about our diverse background, the Anglo-Celtic cultural influence in Australia is still the most dominant of the historical and social influences outlined. Negative attitudes towards Arab and Muslim Australians must be understood in light of these inter-related factors, which include a new resistance to multiculturalism; negative media (mis)representations; educational and social policies (in the form of a folkloric version of cultural diversity); Australia's historical alliance with the Anglo-American, non-Muslim West; as well as the lingering influence of orientalist discourse on perceptions of Islam and the East. In Australia, the situation for Muslims and Arabs has been compounded by current political debates about 'national security' and ongoing public division over the detention of asylum seekers, many of whom are Iraqi and Afghani. As Said proposed, the mere use of the term 'Islam' to either explain or indiscriminately condemn the diverse Islamic world is an irresponsible over-generalisation that is problematic, counterproductive and one that would be unacceptable if applied to any other cultural or demographic group.[2]

This ought to be all the more unacceptable in the context of Australia, which claims to support celebrate its cultural diversity. Nevertheless, since 1997 and Pauline Hanson's reinvigoration of politicised racial conservatism—which, in 2007, she reoriented towards Muslims[3]—national unity has been perceived as compromised by multiculturalism. Little wonder, therefore, that any perceived preferential treatment (*a la* affirmative action) of minority groups rarely garners popular support from a majority of the Australian public. This is evidenced, for example, in the heated debates about Indigenous land rights or economic support directed at particular ethnic groups.[4] Yet, a liberal discourse on equality and equal opportunity (that is, a 'difference-blind' model of multiculturalism) is commonly supported and openly preferred by policy-makers, many groups within civil society, and the general public. Nonetheless, the debate about Muslim integration into Australian society in the current security-conscious political climate still fuels anxieties and xenophobic tendencies.

The recognition of different cultural groups, in particular Muslims and Asians, has been viewed as potentially 'divisive' and, as Pauline Hanson's former party One Nation describes it, as threatening to 'integration and pride in being an Australian'.[5] This conservative populist thinking about multiculturalism and immigration encodes 'the existence of difference within a community ... as disunity, as a pathogen or weakness[6]', and it is this political and social climate that has greeted Islamic migrants to Australia over the last decade. In particular, many Muslims' visibility in a predominantly secular society, has been constructed as a threat to the social homogeneity that was nurtured in Australia until the 1970s. In the age of the 'war on terror', experiments with multiculturalism for the two decades since the mid 1970s have been deemed a dangerous miscalculation by left-leaning 'progressives'. However, the question of whether Australian identity is asserted from its Anglo-Celtic core[7], or whether it is responsive to the realities of cultural diversity, is not of immediate concern to Arab and Muslim Australians. More compelling for this group, under pressure in the current xenophobic social climate, is the desire for social inclusion and recognition of the fundamental citizenship rights that underpin and bind civic identity.[8]

Often the Arab and Muslim migrant experience of detention and strict visa restraints leaves them not only culturally, but socially and economically, marginalised with few points of entry into an often intimidating environment. Some migrants are left to dwell within a sense of dislocation as 'homeless citizens' in exile. As the demonised 'other' becomes more difficult to locate, to identify or to categorise, we become 'trapped inside the fears that politicians inflate', while for some migrants a deepening sense of ambivalence can lead to 'a mixture of slow drift and nervous restlessness'.[9] Nowhere is that sense of drift more potentially corrosive than in young Arab and Muslim Australian students who, as we have described here, can find themselves trapped between the public and private pressures that vie for their identities. A resulting sense of restlessness, and possibly rootlessness, can be managed during the transitional phase of school life, and a sense of belonging retrieved if, as we argue here, a multidimensional responsive approach to education is embraced.

One of the key findings of our research, as discussed in this book, is the importance of holistic, integrative approaches to 'at risk'

Arab and Muslim Australian students, if long-term social integration into the workforce and public life is genuinely the desired outcome. In Australia's increasingly culturally complex school settings, interventions must be flexible enough to take this multidimensional, responsive approach. That is, pedagogical practice and curricular delivery; teacher professional development; student and parent engagement; and building community relationships. Through engaging each of these constituents within the school, its families and its immediate community, they all become stakeholders in the broader and more durable social outcomes.

While discussing the role of education in challenging social and economic inequities is not something new, what this book attempted to do is to locate this endeavour in the context of Arab and Muslim Australian youth in post–September 11 Australia. The approach adopted for the empirical case study reported in this book, the *Diversity Project*, is inspired, if not entirely determined, by aspects of critical race theory. This approach not only recognises social inequalities and economic disadvantages, but more importantly posits a framework for challenging these at the structural, ideological and discursive levels.

In adopting an holistic partnership approach towards analysing cultural diversity and cultural identity among Arab and Muslim Australian students, this book's key objective has been to highlight the many divergent ways by which migrant youth may come to terms with schooling in the context of living between their immigrant heritage and the hegemonic mainstream culture. It has argued, supported by the research data reported in this book, that cultural-identity formation can only be properly understood in individualistic terms. This is because of the multilayered gendered, socio-economic, racial and educational cultural contexts within which migrant youth live, and the varying social and behavioural outcomes engendered by these variables.

This multilayered transformative approach has emphasised the role of quality school–community partnerships and inter-community relations as dynamic constructions that need constant negotiation and structural support. As a perpetual state of becoming 'cultural' and 'intercultural', identity is approached within this study as a process that is navigated within borderless social spaces exhibiting ongoing reflexive cultural transformation.

In reviewing the literature on the management of cultural diversity in schools, this book has also sought to identify the nature of the relationship between migrant youth and the normatively inclusive concepts of multiculturalism, multicultural education and cosmopolitanism. It has found that while multicultural and cosmopolitan approaches to education have at least rhetorically been committed towards combating traditional assimilationist policies and practices by embracing the values of tolerance, understanding and diversity, there has been considerable scholarly criticism of their practical application. Moreover, the terminological shift from the 'old' multicultural to the 'new' intercultural and cosmopolitan seems to have made little impact in terms of redressing the high level of conceptual confusion and lack of innovation among policy-makers and school practitioners alike.

In terms of the literature and the research reported in this book, it has been shown that migrant youth perceptions of multicultural education policies have largely diverged according to the extent to which certain groups feel included or excluded by Australia's cultural mainstream. Migrant groups whose cultural heritage sits comfortably alongside Australia's dominant Anglo-Celtic culture are less likely to criticise existing multicultural policies than those who feel essentialised, 'othered' and excluded from them. It is not surprising, then, that the most vociferous critics of multiculturalism and multicultural education policies are themselves members of the hegemonic mainstream culture. Ironically, this group critiques multiculturalism because it has gone too far towards cultural divisiveness, while minority groups argue that multicultural policies have not gone far enough in terms of cultural rights and equitable social integration.

As the narratives elicited from Arab and Muslim Australian students show, the degree of cultural racialisation in the media can influence young migrant audiences in profound ways. The degree to which migrant youth are attuned to mediated debates about national and international politics shows that even limited messages regarding race and culture may impact upon migrant youth who already feel disconnected from their cultural milieu.

The positive change reported in the attitudinal data reported in this book shows that social and educational intervention can have positive effects if approached from a holistic partnership-based perspective. Education experience, and indeed achievement, can not be looked at in isolation from the immediate social environment within which students, irrespective of their cultural backgrounds, live and interact.

Notes

1   Nikos Papastergiadis, 'The Homeless Citizen', in Cameron McCarthy, Warren Crichlow, Greg Dimistriadis and Nadine Dolby (eds), *Race, Identity, and Representation in Education*, Routledge, New York and London, p. 117.
2   Said, *Covering Islam*, p. xii.
3   In August 2007, Pauline Hanson declared that she was 'sick of Muslims', and urged the Federal Government to curb Australia's intake of Muslim migrants. 'Hanson "Sick of Muslims"', *The Age*, 16 August 2007 and 'Hanson Calls for Halt of Muslim Immigration', *Sydney Morning Herald*, 16 August 2007.
4   See, for example, B Hindess, 1993, 'Multiculturalism and Citizenship', in C Kukathas (ed.), *Multicultural Citizens: The Philosophy and Politics of Identity*, The Centre for Independent Studies Limited, Sydney, p. 34.
5   One Nation policy statement on Multiculturalism and Immigration, http://vic.onenation.com.au/onenation3.1.htm.
6   M Leach, 2000, 'Hansonism, Political Discourse and Australian Identity', in Michael Leach, Geoffrey Stokes and Ian Ward (eds), *The Rise and Fall of One Nation*, University of Queensland Press, Queensland, p. 51.
7   For example, see M Dixson, 1999, *The Imaginary Australian: Anglo-Celts and Identity—1788 to the Present*, UNSW Press, Sydney.
8   G Stokes, 1997, *The Politics of Identity in Australia*, Cambridge University Press, Melbourne.
9   Papastergiadis, p. 133.

References

AAP (Australian Associated Press), 2006, 'Muslims warn of Cronulla-style riots', *The Age*, 1 September.

'The Adelaide Declaration on National Goals for Schooling in the Twenty-first Century', 1999, *10th Ministerial Council on Education, Employment, Training and Youth Affairs (MCEETYA)*, Adelaide, 22–23 April www.dest.gov.au/schools/adelaide/adelaide.htm, viewed 21 October 2008.

Adibi, Hossein, 2003, 'Identity and Cultural Change: The Case of Iranian Youth in Australia', paper presented at the conference 'Social Change in the 21st Century', Centre for Social Change Research, Queensland University of Technology, 21 November.

Akbarzadeh, Shahram and Bianca Smith, 2005, *The Representation of Islam and Muslims in the Media*, Monash University sponsored by The Myer Foundation.

Akermark, Sia Spiliopoulou, 2007, 'Multiculturalism in Crisis?', paper presented at 'III Human Rights Congress – Human Rights in Diversity', Deusto, February.

Aluffi Pentini, Anna, Beatrice Roselletti, Maria Ando, Lucia Tardani, Emilliano Bozzelli, Brigita Zepa, Inese Supule, Nuria Balliu Castanyer, Bru Pellissa, Nils Pagels and Holk Stobbe, *Youth and Inter Ethnic Schools. Actions Against Inter Ethnic Violence among Pupils at School. A Practical Handbook*, p. 42, www.bszi.lv/downloads/resources/DAPHNE/Good%20practices_English.pdf, viewed 18 June 2007.

Anonyuo, Felicia Chigozie, 2006, Agency and Transnationalism: Social Organisation Among Young African Immigrants in the Atlanta Metropolitan Area, MA thesis, Georgia State University, Georgia.

Arvidsson, Adam, 2005, 'What is Culture?', in Karen M Ekstrom and Helene Brembeck (eds), *Elusive Consumption in Retrospect. Report from the Conference*, CFK-Rapport, p. 80, www.hgu.gu.se/files/cfk/rappporter/elusive%20consumption%20in%20retrospect.pdf, viewed 18 June 2007.

Ata, AW 1984, 'Moslem Arab Portrayal in the Australian Press and in School Textbooks', *Australian Journal of Social Issues*, vol. 19, no. 3, pp. 207–17.

The Australian, 2003, 'Gang Rape Reports not Racist: Carr', 21 March.

Australian Bureau of Statistics (ABS), 2001, *2001 Census of Population and Housing*, Australian Bureau of Statistics, Canberra.

——2002, 'Educational Attainment: Literacy and Numeracy Among School Students', in *Australia Now: Australian Social Trends 2002*, Australian Bureau of Statistics, Canberra.

——2003, *2001 Census of Population and Housing: Local Government Area Usual Residence Victoria by Highest Level of Schooling Completed and Age for Language Spoken at Home – Arabic (Including Lebanese)*, Australian Bureau of Statistics, Canberra.

——2004, *Australian Social Trends 2004*, last updated 28 April 2006, www.abs.gov.au, viewed 18 June 2007.

Barton Papers, 1902, Letter from Secretary of the Department of External Affairs, Atlee Hunt, to the Prime Minister, Edmund Barton, on 28 May, 1902, MS 51/1/976, National Library of Australia, Canberra.

Basildon Council, 2006, *'Culture Counts.' A Cultural Strategy for Basildon District*, Essex, United Kingdom, www.basildon.gov.uk/80256B7500420D16/vWeb/flEFEN6U2KQE/$file/basildon+district+council+-+cultural+strategy+2006+-+full+version.pdf, viewed 18 June 2007.

Basit, Tehmina M and Olwen McNamara, 2004, 'Equal Opportunities of Affirmative Action? The Induction of Ethnic Minority Teachers', *Journal of Education for Teaching*, vol. 30, no. 2, pp. 97–116.

Batrouney, Andrew, 2003, 'Arabic Immigration to Australia', paper presented at the conference 'Arabic Smoke Free Sunday', Melbourne, 18 August.

Batrouney, Trevor, 2002, 'From "White Australia" to Multiculturalism: Citizenship and Identity', in Ghassan Hage (ed.), *Arab-Australians Today: Citizenship and Belonging*, Melbourne University Press, Melbourne, pp. 37–62.

Bauman, Z, 2001, 'The Great War of Recognition', *Theory, Culture and Society*, vol. 18, nos 2–3, pp. 137–50.

Berk, Laura E. 1997, *Child Development*, Allyn & Bacon, Boston.

Berry, John W, 2006, *Breakfast on the Hill. Petit Dejeuner sur la Colline. Fitting In: A Place for Immigrant Teens in Canadian Society*, Canadian Federation for the Humanities and Social Sciences, Ottawa.

Bhui, Kamaldeep, Stephen Stansfeld, Jenny Head, Mary Haines, Sheila Hillier, Stephanie Taylor, Russell Viner and Robert Booy, 2005, 'Cultural Identity, Acculturation and Mental Health Among Adolescents in East London's Multiethnic Community', *Journal of Epidemiology and Community Health*, vol. 59, pp. 296–302.

Bolt, A, 2002, 'Schooled to Fail', *Herald Sun*, 16 December.

——2004, 'A Culture in Crisis', *Herald Sun*, 15 September.

——2004, 'Moaners Strangle a School', *Herald Sun*, 1 August.

Buckley, Siddiq, 2005, 'Australian Muslims: Alert and Alarmed!', *Salam Magazine*, 26 November, Federation of Australian Muslim Students and Youth Inc, www.famsy.com/famsy/modules/smartsection/item.php?itemid=21&keywords=Australian+Muslims:+Alert+and+Alarmed, viewed 18 June 2007.

Burchell, David, 2006, 'An Email from the Ether: After the Cronulla Events', *Australian Universities Review*, vol. 48, no. 2, pp. 6–8.

Butcher, Melissa, 2004, 'Universal Processes of Cultural Change: Reflections on the Identity Strategies of Indian and Australian Youth', *Journal of Intercultural Studies*, vol. 25, no. 3, pp. 215–31.

Butcher, M and M Thomas 2001, *GENERATE: Youth Culture and Migration Heritage in Western Sydney*, Institute for Cultural Research, University of Western Sydney and Migration Heritage Centre, Sydney.

Cafagna, Josephine, Teresa Crea, Anna Maria Dell'oso, Melina Marchetta, Maria Pallotta-Chiarolli and Virginia Trioli, 2000, *Panel Discussion on Exploring Identity and Community through the Arts and Culture*, 25 May, p. 806, www.iai.com.au/Exploring%20Identity.pdf, viewed 18 June 2007.

Cahill, D, 1996, *Immigration and Schooling in the 1990s*, Australian Government Publishing Service, Canberra.

Chae, Hui Soo, 2003, 'Talking Back to the Asian Model Minority Discourse: Korean-Origin Youth Experiences in High School', *Journal of Intercultural Studies*, vol. 25, no. 1, pp. 59–73.

Chao, Georgia T and Henry Moon, 2005, 'The Cultural Mosaic: A Metatheory for Understanding the Complexity of Culture', *Journal of Applied Psychology*, vol. 90, no. 6, pp. 1128–40.

Chen, Tsai-Wei, 2006, 'Sonic Constellations: Taiwanese Sojourners' Listening Experiences in London', *Organised Sound*, vol. 11, no. 1, pp. 37–44.

Chomsky, Noam, 2001, *September 11*, Allen & Unwin, USA and Australia.

——2003, *Power and Terror: Post-9/11 Talks and Interviews*, Seven Stories Press, New York.

Cleland, Bilal, 2001, 'Spreading the Message of Islam in Anglo-Australia: Developing a Positive Image for Islam in Australia', *Salam Magazine*, 26 November, Federation of Australian Muslim Students and Youth Inc. (Part Two of a lecture presented on the 3 March, Curtin University, Perth. Organised by FAMSY (WA) and CMSA (Curtin University MSA)), www.famsy.com/salam/IslamOz61.htm, viewed 1 June 2006.

Crittenden, Stephen, 2006, Interview Dr Ameer Ali, Chairman of the Muslim Reference Group, and Dr Tanveer Ahmed, psychiatrist, *Religion Report*, ABC Radio National, 6 September.

Clancy, Emma, 2003, 'Carr Government Bans Student Peace March', *Green Left Weekly*, 2 April, www.greenleft.org.au/back/2003/532, viewed 18 June 2007.

——2003, 'Sorry to disappoint the media', *Green Left Weekly*, 9 April, www.greenleft.org.au/2003/533/30514, viewed 18 June 2007.

CNN World 2001, 'You Are Either With Us or Against Us in the Fight Against Terror', *CNN.com World*, 6 November, http://archives.cnn.com/2001/US/11/06/gen.attack.on.terror/, viewed 22 October 2008.

——2002, 'Record Rape Sentence Rocks Australia', *CNN.com World*, 16 August, www.cnn.com/2002/WORLD/asiapcf/auspac/08/16/australia.legal/, viewed 18 June 2007.

Connell, RW, 2003, *The Role of Men and Boys in Achieving Gender Equality*, United Nations Division for the Advancement of Women (DAW) in collaboration with International Labour Organisation (ILO), the Joint United Nations Programmes on HIV/AIDS (UNAIDS) and the United Nations Development Programme (UNPD), Brasilia, Brazil, 7 October.

Considine, G and G Zappalà, 2002, 'Factors Influencing the Educational Performance of Students from Disadvantaged Backgrounds', in T Eardley and B Bradley (eds), *Competing Visions: Refereed Proceedings of the National Social Policy Conference 2001*, SPRC Report 1/02, University of New South Wales, Sydney, pp. 91–107.

Colic-Peisker, Val and Farida Tilbury, 2007, *Refugees and Employment: The Effect of Visible Difference on Discrimination*, Final Report, Centre for Social and Community Research, Murdoch University, Perth.

Collins, J, G Noble, S Poynting and P Tabar, 2000, *Kebabs, Kids, Cops and Crime: Ethnicity, Youth and Crime*, Pluto Press Australia, Annandale.

Coulby, David, 2006, 'Intercultural Education: Theory and Practice', *Intercultural Education*, vol. 17, no. 3, pp. 245–57.

The Daily Telegraph, 2003, 'General Comments on War Issues', 27 March.

Das, Sushi, 2003, 'Young Muslims: Torn Between Two Cultures', *The Age*, 15 March.

Deen, H, 2003, *Caravanserai: Journey Among Australian Muslims*, Fremantle Arts Centre Press, Fremantle.

De Castro, Rui Vieira, Paula Guimarces and Amelia Vitoria Sancho, 2006, 'Contributions to the Outline of a Training Device for Adult Educators', in Tiina Jaager and John Irons (eds), *Towards Becoming a Good Adult Educator – A Recourse Book for Adult Educators*, AGADE, Budapest, pp. 17–22.

De Haan, Mariette and Ed Elbers, 2004, 'Minority Status and Culture: Local Constructions of Diversity in a Classroom in the Netherlands', *Intercultural Education*, vol. 15, no. 4, pp. 441–53.

Department of Education, Science and Training, 1998, *Discovering Democracy Units*, Commonwealth of Australia, DEST, www.curriculum.edu.au/ddunits/units/ms5fq2acts.htm#Activity%207, viewed 18 June 2007.

Department of Immigration and Citizenship, 2007, *Muslims in Australia— A Snapshot*, Australian Government, DIAC, www.immi.gov.au/living-in-australia/a-diverse-australia/communities/muslim-community/conference-Australian_Imams/Muslims_in_Australia_snapshot.pdf, viewed 18 June 2007.

——*Muslims in Australia—A Snapshot*, Australian Government, DIAC, http://www.immi.gov.au/media/publications/multicultural/pdf_doc/Muslims_in_Australia_snapshot.pdf

——2007, *Fact Sheet 75. Processing Unlawful Boat Arrivals*, Australian Government, DIAC, www.immi.gov.au/media/fact-sheets/75processing.htm, viewed 18 June 2007.

Devine, Dympna and Mary Kelly, 2006, '"I Just Don't Want to Get Picked on by Anybody": Dynamics of Inclusion and Exclusion in a Newly Multi-Ethnic Irish Primary School', *Children & Society*, vol. 20, no. 2, pp. 128–39.

Dietz, Gunther, 2004, 'Frontier Hybridisation or Culture Clash? Transnational Migrant Communities and Sub-National Identity Politics in Andalusia, Spain', *Journal of Ethnic and Migration Studies*, vol. 30, no. 6, pp. 1087–112.

Dixson, M, 1999, *The Imaginary Australian: Anglo-Celts and Identity–1788 to the Present*, UNSW Press, Sydney.

Dobson, I, B Birrell and V Rapson, 1996, 'The Participation of Non-English-Speaking-Background Person in Higher Education', *People and Place*, vol. 4, no. 1, pp. 46–54.

Dobson, I, R Sharma and A Haydon, 1996, *Evaluation of the Relative Performance of Commencing Undergraduate Students in Australian Universities*, Australian Credit Transfer Agency, Adelaide.

Duffy, Daniel, 2006, 'Autonomy, Representation and *Lekil Kuxlejal* in Highland Chiapas', in *Alone With Five Others: Dispatches from a Changing World*, The International Centre for Ethics, Justice and Public Life, Brandeis University, www.brandeis.edu/ethics/publications/ECSF_06.pdf, viewed 18 June 2007.

Duhou, IA and R Teese, 1992, *Education, Work Force and Community Participation of Arab Australians: Egyptians, Lebanese, Palestinians and Syrians*, Australian Government Publishing Service, Canberra.

Dunn, KM, 1998, 'Rethinking Ethnic Concentration: Cabramatta, The Case of Sydney', *Urban Studies*, vol. 35, no. 3, pp. 503–27.

——2003, 'Racism in Australia: Findings of a Survey on Racist Attitudes and Experiences of Racism', National Europe Centre Paper No. 77 presented at the conference 'The Challenges of Immigration and Integration in the European Union and Australia', University of Sydney, Sydney, 18–20 February.

Dunn, KM, V Gandhi, I Burnley and J Forrest, 2003, 'Racism in Australia: Cultural Imperialism, Disempowerment and Violence', in J Gao J, R Le Heron and J Logie (eds), *Windows on a Changing World: Proceedings of the 22nd New Zealand Geographical Society Conference*, New Zealand Geographical Society, Auckland, pp. 180–3.

Dunn, Lee and Michelle Wallace, 2006, 'Australian Academics and Transnational Teaching: An Exploratory Study of Their Preparedness and Experiences', *Higher Education and Research Development*, vol. 25, no. 4, pp. 357–69.

Echberg, K, 2004, 'Sad End to a School with a Proud and Vibrant Past', *The Age*, 4 August.

Editorial, 2004, 'Sacrificing Schools to the Numbers Game', *The Age*, 4 August.

Edelman, M, 2001, *The Politics of Disinformation*, Cambridge University Press, Cambridge.

Elsden-Clifton, Jennifer, 2006, 'Constructing "Thirdspaces": Migrant Students and the Visual Arts', *Studies in Learning, Evaluation, Innovation and Development*, vol. 3, no. 1, pp. 1–11.

Feinberg, Ben, 2006, 'The Promise and Peril of Public Anthropology', *Human Rights & Human Welfare*, vol. 6, pp. 165–77.

Fernández-Kelly, P Konczal and L Konczal, 2005, 'Murdering the Alphabet – Identity and Entrepreneurship among Second Generation Cubans, West Indians, and Central Americans', *Ethnic and Racial Studies*, vol. 28, no. 6, pp. 1153–81.

Foster, Victoria, 1998, *Gender, Schooling Achievement and Post-School Pathways: Beyond Statistics and Populist Discourse*, paper presented at the Australian Association for Research and Education, Adelaide, December.

Franchi, Vije and Anne Andronikof-Sanglade, 2001, 'Intercultural Identity Structure of Second Generation French Women of African Descent', in Simon Bekker, Martine Dodds and Meshack M Khosa (eds), *Shifting African Identities*, Identity? Theory, Politics, History, Human Sciences Research Council, Pretoria, pp. 115–32.

Friedman, Victor J and Ariane Berthoin Antal, 2005, 'Negotiating Reality: A Theory of Action Approach to Intercultural Competence', *Management Learning*, vol. 36, no. 1, pp. 69–86.

Ghaffar-Kucher, Ameena, 2006, 'Assimilation, Integration and Isolation? (Re)framing the Education of Immigrants', *Current Issues in Comparative Education*, Teachers College, University of Columbia, www.tc.columbia. edu/cice/Current/9.1/91_edintro.html, viewed 18 June 2007.

Gibbons, J, W White and P Gibbons, 1994, 'Combating Educational Disadvantage among Lebanese Australians', in T Skutnabb-Kangas and R Phillipson in collaboration with M Rannut (eds), *Linguistic Human Rights: Overcoming Linguistic Disadvantage*, Mouton de Gruye, Berlin, pp. 253–64.

Gibson, Margaret A, 2005, 'Promoting Academic Engagement among Minority Youth: Implications from John Ogbu's Shaker Heights Ethnography', *International Journal of Qualitative Studies in Education*, vol. 18, no. 5, pp. 581–603.

Gordon. Josh and Jewel Tospfield, 2006, 'Our Values or Go Home: Costello', *The Age*, 24 February.

Grattan, Michelle, 2005, 'Accept Australian Values or Get Out', *The Australian*, 25 August.

Grenfell, Michael, 2004, *Pierre Bourdieu, Agent Provocateur*, Continuum, London and New York.

Green, S, 2004, 'Troubled School Shuts Door', *The Age*, 31 July.

Greer, Anne and Wenh In Ng, 2004, 'Beyond Bible Stories: The Role of Culture Specific Myths/Stories in the Identity Formation of Nondominant Immigrant Children', *Religious Education*, vol. 99, no. 2, pp. 125–36.

Hage, Ghassan, 2003, *Against Paranoid Nationalism: Searching for Hope in a Shrinking Society*, Pluto Press, Australia.

——2002, 'Citizenship and Honourability: Belonging to Australia Today', in Ghassan Hage (ed.), *Arab-Australians Today: Citizenship and Belonging*, Melbourne University Press, Melbourne, pp. 1–15.

——2002, 'Postscript: Arab-Australian belonging after "September 11"' in Ghassan Hage (ed.), *Arab-Australians Today: Citizenship and Belonging*, Melbourne University Press, Melbourne, pp. 241–8.

Harris, Trudy, 2005, 'Children Exported as Brides', *The Australian*, 2 August.

Harvey, Jim, 1996, 'Distance, Isolation and Place: A Study of Youth Living in a Remote Mining Community', paper presented at the conference 'Educational Research: Building New Partnerships (ERA: AARE)', Singapore, 25–29 November.

Herald Sun, 2004, 'School Closure "Right Thing to Do"', 31 July.

Herrera, Diego, 2003, 'School Success of Moroccan Youth in Barcelona: Theoretical Insights for Practical Questions', *Anthenea Digital*, vol. 4, pp. 97–108.

Hindess, B, 1993, 'Multiculturalism and Citizenship', in C Kukathas (ed), *Multicultural Citizens: The Philosophy and Politics of Identity*, The Centre for Independent Studies Limited, Sydney, pp. 31–45.

Hollinsworth, David, 1998, *Race and Racism in Australia*, Social Science Press, Sydney.

Horvath, B, 1987, 'VARBRUL Analysis in Applied Linguistics: A Case Study', *Australian Review of Applied Linguistics*, vol. 10, no. 2, pp. 59–67.

Human Rights and Equal Opportunity Commission (HREOC), 2003, *Fact Sheet: Australians of Arab, Middle Eastern and North African Birth and Ancestry*, 21 March.

——2004, *Isma—Listen: National Consultations on Eliminating Prejudice Against Arab and Muslim Australians: Final Report*, Human Rights and Equal Opportunity Commission, Sydney, June, http://www.humanrights. gov.au/racial_discrimination/isma/index.html/, viewed 10 November 2008.

——2005, *Fact Sheet: Australians of Arab, Middle Eastern and North African Birth and Ancestry*, 16 June, www.hreoc.gov.au/racial_discrimination/ isma/consultations/facts/fact_arab.html, viewed 18 June 2007.

Huntington, Samuel P, 2002, *The Clash of Civilizations and the Remaking of the World Order*, Simon & Schuster, London.

International Youth Summit, 2001, *United to Combat Racism: A Youth Vision! Final Declaration and Plan of Action*, Durban South Africa, 26 August – 8 September.

Jamal, Nadia and Taghred Chandah, 2005, *The Glory Garage: Growing up Lebanese Muslim in Australia*, Allen & Unwin, Sydney.

Jureidini, Ray and Ghassan Hage, 2002, 'The Australian Arabic Council: Anti-Racist Activism', in Ghassan Hage (ed), *Arab-Australians Today: Citizenship and Belonging*, Melbourne University Press, Melbourne, pp. 173–91.

Keller, Ursula, 2006, *Post-Secondary Educational Attainment of Immigrant and Native Youth*, Centre for Demography and Population Health, University of Florida.

Kennedy, M, 2000, 'Arabic-Speaking Young People, the Police and the Media', in J Collins and S Poynting (eds), *The Other Sydney: Communities, Identities and Inequalities in Western Sydney*, Common Ground Publishing, Melbourne, pp. 79–105.

Kenny, S, F Mansouri and P Spratt, 2005, *Arabic Communities and Well-Being: Supports and Barriers to Social Connectedness*, Centre For Citizenship & Human Rights (CCHR), Deakin University, Geelong.

Kerbaj, Richard, 2006, 'PM tells Muslims to Learn English', *The Australian*, 1 September.

Kerbaj, R and M Chulov, 2007, 'Australia's Home-Grown Jihad Threat', *The Australian*, 2 July.

Khanlou, Nazilla, 2005, 'Cultural Identity as Part of Youth's Self-Concept in Multicultural Settings', *International Journal of Mental Health and Addiction*, vol. 3, no. 2, pp. 1–14.

Khoo, S-E, P McDonald, D Giorgas and B Birrell, 2002, *Second Generation Australians: Report for the Department of Immigration and Multicultural and Indigenous Affairs*, Department of Immigration and Multicultural and Indigenous Affairs, Canberra, April, www.immi.gov.au/media/publications/multicultural/2gen/index.htm, viewed 18 June 2007.

Kingston, M, 2003, 'Howard's Case: The Missing Links', *Sydney Morning Herald*, 5 February.

Knowles, Elanor and Wendy Ridley, 2006, *Another Spanner in the Works: Challenging Prejudice and Racism in Mainly White Schools*, Trentham Books Limited, Oakhill, England, and Stirling, USA.

Le Roux, J, 2001, 'Social Dynamics of the Multicultural Classroom', *Intercultural Education*, vol. 12, no. 3, pp. 273–88.

Leach, M, 2000, 'Hansonism, Political Discourse and Australian Identity', in Michael Leach, Geoffrey Stokes and Ian Ward (eds), *The Rise and Fall of One Nation*, University of Queensland Press, Queensland, pp. 42–56.

Lee, Jennifer Wenshya and Yvonne M Hebert, 2006, 'The Meaning of Being Canadian: A Comparison Between Youth of Immigrant and Non-Immigrant Origins', *Canadian Journal of Education*, vol. 29, no. 2, pp. 497–520.

Lee, Richard, 2005, *Youth, Citizenship and Modern Society: A Study of the Engaging Young People Project in East Cleveland*, Working Paper No. 75, Centre for Rural Economy, University of Newcastle Upon Tyne, UK.

Leeman, YAM, 2003, 'School Leadership for Intercultural Education', *Intercultural Education*, vol. 14, no. 1, pp. 31–46.

Leeman, Yvonne and Guuske Ledoux, 2003, 'Intercultural Education in Dutch Schools', *Curriculum Inquiry*, vol. 33, no. 4, pp. 385–99.

Liebkind, Karmela, Inga Jasinskaja-Lahti and Erling Solheim, 2004, 'Cultural Identity, Perceived Discrimination, and Parental Support as Determinants of Immigrants' School Adjustments: Vietnamese Youth in Finland', *Journal of Adolescent Research*, vol. 19, no. 6, pp. 635–56.

Local Learning and Employment Network (LLEN), 2004, *On Track 2004*, Department of Education and Training, Victoria.

Luchtenberg, Sigrid, 1998, 'Identity Education in Multicultural Germany', *Journal of Multilingual and Multicultural Development*, vol. 19, no. 1, pp. 51–63.

Malabotta, Melita Richter, 2005, 'Managing Cultural Transitions: Multiculturalism, Interculturalism and Minority Policies', in Nada

Svob-Dokic (ed), *The Emerging Creative Industries in Southern Europe*, Institute for International Relations, Zagreb, pp. 167–77.

Mansouri, Fethi, 2004, 'Race, Identity and Education Achievements among Arab-Australians Students', paper presented at the 'Eleventh International Learning Conference', Havana, Cuba, 27–30 June.

Mansouri, Fethi and Anna Trembath, 2005, 'Multicultural Education and Racism: The Case of Arab-Australian Students in Contemporary Australia', *International Education Journal*, vol. 6, no. 4, pp. 516–29.

Mansouri, Fethi, 2005, 'Citizenship, Identity and Belonging in Contemporary Australia', in S Akbarzadeh and S Yasmeen (eds), *Islam and the West: Reflections from Australia*, UNSW Press, Sydney, pp. 114–32.

Mansouri, M and C Makhoul, 2004, *Arab-Australians in Victoria: Needs Assessment and Community Capacity Building*, Centre for Citizenship and Human Rights, Deakin University, Geelong.

Marti, Josep, 2005, 'The *Cultural Frames* Approach as an Alternative to the Ethnocratic Idea of Culture', Spanish Council for Scientific Research, www.anthroglobe.ca/docs/Cultural-Frames-as-Alternative-to-%20Ethnocratic-Idea-Culture.htm, last edited 23 September 2005, viewed 18 June 2007.

Martino, Wayne and Bob Meyenn, 2001, 'Preface', in Wayne Martino and Bob Meyenn (eds), *What about the Boys? Issues of Masculinity in Schools*, Open University Press, Buckingham and Philadelphia, pp. xi–xiv.

Matthews, Zachariah, 2005, 'Unity in the Face of Adversity', *Salam Magazine*, 26 November, Federation of Australian Muslim Students and Youth Inc, paper presented at the Islamic Legal fund launch on 2 July 2004, www.famsy.com/famsy/modules/smartsection/item.php?itemid=22, viewed 18 June 2007.

McDonell, Stephen, 2002, Interview with Dr Ghassan Hage, *Four Corners*, Australian Broadcasting Corporation, 26 August, www.abc.net.au/4corners/stories/s677558.htm, viewed 18 June 2007.

McIlvean, L, 2006, 'Young Muslim Leader Backs Howard', *Daily Telegraph*, 5 September.

Meade, P, 1983, *The Educational Experiences of Sydney High Schools Students Report No. 3: A Comparative Study of Migrant Students of Non-English-Speaking Origin and Students Whose Parents were Born in an English-Speaking Country*, vol. 3, Australian Government Publishing Service, Canberra.

Megalogenis, George, 2002, 'Multicultural Australia Examined: The Full-Text of the John Howard Interview', *The Australian*, 6 February.

Merry, Michael S, 2005, 'Social Exclusion of Muslim Youth in Flemish and French-Speaking Schools', *Comparative Education Review*, vol. 49, no. 1, pp. 1–22.

Miller, Mark J, 2006, *Opportunities and Challenges for Migrant and Migrant-Background Youth in Developed Countries*, short version report submitted to the United Nations Social and Economic Council, 15 July.

Monawar, Abed, 2006, Cultural Assimilation Among Palestinian Immigrants in New Mexico, MA thesis, Texas Technical University, Texas.

Morin, Edgar, 2006, 'Speech', in *What UNESCO for the Future? Forum of Reflexion*, Social and Human Sciences Sector, The United Nations Educational, Scientific and Cultural Organisation, Paris, pp. 27–33.

Nader, C, 2002, 'Muslim Students Brace for Unwanted Anniversary', *The Age*, 5 September.

Nahlous, Lena, 2001, 'Women, Violence and the Media', paper presented at the conference 'Women Reporting Violence in a Time of War', Sydney University of Technology, 8 November, http://international.activism.hss. uts.edu.au/conferences/w_violence/transcripts/nahlous.html, viewed 18 June 2007.

Noble, Greg and Scott Poynting, 2003, 'Acts of War: Military Metaphors in Representations of Lebanese Youth Gangs', *Media International Australia Incorporating Culture and Policy*, no. 106, pp. 110–23.

Noble, Greg, Scott Poynting and Paul Tabar, 1999, 'Youth, Ethnicity and the Mapping of Identities: Strategic Essentialism and Strategic Hybridity among Male Arabic-Speaking Youth in South-Western Sydney', *Communal/Plural*, vol. 7, no. 1, pp. 29–44.

Novick, Rebecca, 1999, *Family Involvement & Beyond. School-Based Child and Family Support Programs*, Northwest Regional Educational Laboratory, Portland.

Nussbaum, Martha C , 'Patriotism and Cosmopolitanism' in Joshua Cohen (ed), *For Love of Country: Debating the Limits of Patriotism*, Beacon Press, Boston, 1996, pp. 3–17.

Ochocka, Joanna et al, 2006, *Pathways to Success. Immigrant Youth at High School*, Centre for Research and Education in Human Services, Wilfrid Laurier University, Ontario.

Omar, Wafia and Kirsty Allen, 1997, *The Muslims in Australia*, Australian Government Printing Service, Canberra.

Padilla, Amado M, 2006, 'Bicultural Social Development', *Hispanic Journal of Behavioural Sciences*, vol. 28, no. 4, pp. 467–97.

Page, Bryan, 2005, 'The Concept of Culture: A Core Issue in Health Disparities', *Journal of Urban Health: Bulletin of the New York Academy of Medicine*, vol. 82, no. 2, Supplement 3.

Park, Yoosun, 2005, 'Culture as Deficit: A Critical Analysis of the Concept of Culture in Contemporary Social Work Discourse', *Journal of Sociology and Social Welfare*, online article 1 September 2005.

Perreira, Krista M, Kathleen Mullan Harris and Doohan Lee, 2006, 'Making it in America: High School Completion by Immigrant and Native Youth', *Demography*, vol. 43, no. 3, pp. 511–36.

Poynting, Scott and Greg Noble, 2004, *Living with Racism: The Experience and Reporting by Arab and Muslim Australians of Discrimination, Abuse and Violence Since 11 September 2001*, Report to The Human Rights and Equal Opportunity Commission, 19 April, www.hreoc.gov.au/racial_ discrimination/isma/research/index.html, viewed 18 June 2007.

Poynting, Scott, Greg Noble and Paul Tabar, 1999, '"Intersections" of Masculinity and Ethnicity: A Study of Male Lebanese Immigrant Youth in Western Sydney', *Race Ethnicity and Education*, vol. 2, no. 1, pp. 59–77.

Poynting, Scott, Greg Noble, Paul Tabar and Jock Collins, 2004, *Bin Laden in the Suburbs: Criminalising the Arab Other*, Sydney Institute of Criminology Series, Sydney.

Poynting, Scott and Paul Tabar, 2002, 'On Being Lebanese-Australian: Hybridity, Essentialism and Strategy among Arabic-Speaking Youth', in Ghassan Hage (ed.), *Arab-Australians Today: Citizenship and Belonging*, Melbourne University Press, Melbourne, pp.128–44.

Pratt, Geraldine, 2002, *Between Homes: Displacement and Belonging for Second Generation Filipina-Canadian Youths*, Research on Immigration and Integration in the Metropolis Working Paper Series no. 2–13, Vancouver Centre of Excellence, Vancouver.

Prieur, Annick, 2002, 'Gender Remix: On Gender Constructions among Children of Immigrants in Norway', *Ethnicities*, vol. 2, no. 1, pp. 53–77.

Pries, L, 2003, 'Labour Migration, Social Incorporation and Transmigration in the Old and New Europe: The Case Germany in a Comparative Perspective', *Transfer*, vol. 9, no. 3, pp. 432–51.

Qin, Desiree Baolian, 2006, 'The Role of Gender in Immigrant Children's Educational Adaptation', *Current Issues in Comparative Education*, vol. 9, no. 1, pp. 8–19.

Research Utilisation Support and Help (RUSH), 1999, *Disability, Diversity, and Dissemination. A Review of the Literature on Topics Related to Increasing the Utilisation of Rehabilitation Research Outcomes among Diverse Consumer Groups*, April www.researchutilization.org/matrix/resources/ddd/DisabilityDiversity.pdf, viewed 18 June 2007.

Robb, Andrew, 2006, 'Opening Address', paper presented at the 'Adult Migrant English Program National Conference – Cultures of Learning', Perth, 5 October, www.minister.immi.gov.au/parlsec/media/speeches/cultures_learning.htm, viewed 18 June 2007.

Rothman, S and J McMillan, 2003, *Longitudinal Surveys of Australian Youth Research Report 36: Influences on Achievement in Literacy and Numeracy*, Australian Council for Educational Research, Melbourne.

Rumbaut, Ruben G, 1994, 'The Crucible Within: Ethnic Identity, Self-Esteem and Segmented Assimilation among Children of Immigrants', *International Migration Review*, vol. 28, pp. 748–94.

Saeed, Abdullah, 2003, *Islam in Australia*, Allen & Unwin, Sydney.

Saeed, Abdullah and Shahram Akbarzadeh, 2001, *Muslim communities in Australia*, UNSW Press, Sydney.

Said, Edward W, 1978, *Orientalism: Western Conceptions of the Orient*, Penguin Books, London.

——1997, *Covering Islam: How the Media and the Experts Determine How We See the Rest of the World*, Vintage Books, London.

Shonkoff, JP and DA Phillips (eds), 2000, *From Neurons to Neighborhoods*, National Academy Press, Washington DC.

Sieber, Timothy, 2005, 'Popular Music and Cultural Identity in the Cape Verdean Post-Colonial Diaspora', *Ethnographica*, vol. IX, no. 1, pp. 123–48.

Somnath, Saha, 2006, 'The Relevance of Cultural Distance Between Patients and Physicians to Racial Disparities in Health Care', *Journal of General Internal Medicine*, vol. 21, no. 2, pp. 203–5.

Stevens, C, 1989, *Tin Mosques & Ghantowns: A History of Afghan Camel Drivers in Australia*, Oxford University Press, Melbourne.

Stevenson, Nick, 2003, 'Cultural Citizenship in the "Cultural" Society: A Cosmopolitan Approach', *Citizenship Studies*, vol. 7, no. 3, pp. 331–48.

Stivachtis, Yannis A, 2006, 'The International Order in a Multicultural World: Challenges for the "International" University', paper presented at the '3rd Mid Atlantic Conference on the Scholarship of Diversity', Blacksburg, Virginia, 2–3 February.

Stokes, G, 1997, *The Politics of Identity in Australia*, Cambridge University Press, Melbourne.

Student Outcomes Division, Department of Education & Training, 2003, *Annual Report 2002*, State Government of Victoria, Melbourne.

——2004, *2004 School Census—Language Background Other than English students*, State Government of Victoria, Melbourne.

Suarez-Orozco, Carola, 2003, 'Formulating Identity in a Globalised World', in Marcelo M Suarez-Orozco and Desiree Qin-Hilliard (eds), *Globalisation: Culture and Education in the New Millennium*, University of California Press and Ross Institute, California, pp.173–202.

Suarez-Orozco, Carola and Desiree Baolian Qin-Hilliard, 2003, 'Immigrant Boys' Experiences in US Schools', in Niobe Way and Judy Y Chu (eds), *Adolescent Boys in Context*, New York University Press, New York, pp. 345–58.

Suliman, R and DM McInerney, 2003, 'Motivational Goals and School Achievement: Lebanese-Background Students in South-Western Sydney', paper presented at 'Australian Association for Research in Education/New Zealand Association for Research in Education Joint Conference', Auckland, New Zealand, November 2003.

Surbone, Antonella, 2004, 'Cultural Competence: Why?', *Annals of Oncology*, vol. 15, pp. 697–9.

Swanson Dena Phillips , Margaret Beale Spencer, Vinay Harpalani, Davido Dupree, Elizabeth Noll, Sofia Ginzburg and Gregory Seaton, 2003, 'Psychosocial Development in Racially and Ethnically Diverse Youth: Conceptual and Methodological Challenges in the 21st Century', *Development and Psychopathology*, vol. 15.

Tavan, Gwenda, 2005, *The Long, Slow Death of White Australia*, Scribe Publications, Melbourne.

Vaquera, Elizabeth and Grace Kao, 2006, 'The Implications of Choosing "No Race" on the Salience of Hispanic Identity: How Racial and Ethnic Backgrounds Intersect Among Hispanic Adolescents', *The Sociological Quarterly*, vol. 47, pp. 375–96.

Vedder, P, G Horenczyk and K Liebkind, 2006, *Ethno-Culturally Diverse Education Settings: Problems, Challenges and Solutions*, European Association for Research on Learning and Instruction, p. 6, www.earli.org/resources/Position%20Paper%202%20Ethno-culturally%20diverse%20education%20settings.pdf, viewed 18 June 2007.

Victorian Office of Multicultural Affairs (VOMA), 2003, *Victorian Community Profiles 2001 Census Summary Statistics: Lebanon-Born*, State Government of Victoria, Melbourne, www.voma.vic.gov.au/domino/web_notes/voma/vomasite.nsf, viewed 21 October 2008.

Vo, An, 2003, *Don't Throw Another Shrimp on the Barbie or Cultural Identity Matters,!* www.thesource.gov.au/involve/NYR/word/reports_social/a_vo.doc, viewed 18 June 2007.

Waitt, Gordon, Rebecca M Galea and Patrick Rawstone, 2001, 'Generation and Place of Residence in the Symbolic and Lived Identity of Maltese in Sydney, Australia', *Australian Geographer*, vol. 32, no. 1, pp. 77–91.

Wakholi, Peter, 2005, African Cultural Education: A Dialogue with African Migrant Youth in Western Australia, MEd thesis, Murdoch University, Perth.

Walker, Jeffrey P and Ana M Serrano, 2006, 'Formulating a Cosmopolitan Approach to Immigration and Social Policy: Lessons from American (North and South) Indigenous and Immigrant Groups', *Current Issues in Comparative Education*, vol. 9, no. 1, pp. 60–8.

Wedeen, Lisa, 2002, 'Conceptualising Culture: Possibilities for Political Science', *American Political Science Review*, vol. 96, no. 4, pp. 713–28.

White, P, 2004, 'Media Savages Lebanese-Australian Youth', *On Line Opinion: Australia's e-Journal of Social and Political Debate*, 15 September, www.onlineopinion.com.au/view.asp?article=2552, viewed 18 June 2007.

Worbs, S, 2003, 'The Second Generation in Germany: Between School and Labor Market', *International Migration Review*, vol. 37, no. 4, pp. 1011–38.

Young, C, M Petty and A Faulkner, 1980, *Education and Employment of Turkish and Lebanese Youth*, Australian Government Publishing Service, Canberra.

Index

Printed and bound by CPI Group (UK) Ltd, Croydon, CR0 4YY

07/07/2026

14916232-0001